W9-AXJ-902

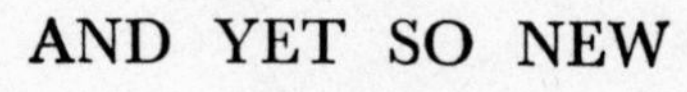

AND YET SO NEW

AND YET SO NEW

by

ARNOLD LUNN

Late have I loved thee, thou Beauty
so old and yet so new.

St. Augustine

SHEED & WARD · NEW YORK

Library of Congress Catalog Card Number 58-14453

We wish to express our thanks to *The Critic* for permitting us to reprint part of the chapter "Memories of Hilaire Belloc."

Manufactured in the United States of America

FOREWORD

TO GEORGE COOPER

My dear George,

It was in 1944 that a young American diplomat bought a book in Burns and Oates' on his way back to the flat which he had leased for the War. The temperamental lift stopped on the floor below his flat, a fact which he only realized when he saw not his own name on a visiting card pinned onto the door of the flat, but the name of the author whose book he had just bought. And that is how we met.

We have met many times since the temperamental lift brought us together; in America at Trinity College, Hartford, after you had transferred from the Foreign Service and embarked on an academic career, in Zermatt by a lucky chance last summer, and in London during your sabbatical year.

I first visited your country in 1935, and spent some months in America during the most anxious period of the War. I was heartened in those dark days by the energy of all those who were campaigning for the American intervention which alone could have saved Europe from Nazi domination, and I remember with particular gratitude the Americans who gave time and money to provide "Bundles for Britain". Only those who were in London during the Blitz can fully appreciate what those bundles meant to our stricken people. Then, as now, there were many American homes whose threshold I never crossed without a sense of escape from temporal worries. It is almost trite to pay a tribute to American hospitality, but only those who have experienced it can properly appreciate its quality.

I am grateful to you for many kindnesses and also, as an Englishman, for all that you have done for Anglo-American relations. I enjoyed your story of the irreverent undergraduate who arranged for a telegram to be delivered to you just as you were opening a debate on what should be America's attitude to England: "Keep up the good work. Cheque follows. Selwyn Lloyd."

Since I first visited your country there has been a sharp decline in the number of embittered Anglophobes, and there has been a corresponding decline in my country of their opposite numbers. And even those who are still prejudiced against their allies on the other side of the Atlantic must realize, if they have any sense of responsibility, that Soviet Russia is the only beneficiary of anything which weakens the free world. We Catholics, who belong to a universal Church, have even less excuse than other people for such parochial vendettas, for every advance of the Communists drives more Catholics into the catacombs, and for this, if for no other reason, we must try not only to forgive our enemies but also our allies.

It is less easy for the untravelled, who have never crossed or approached the frontier of fear which separates the world which is still free from the world which is enslaved, fully to realize the perilous position of Christendom today. Missionaries have fewer illusions on this point than other people. I remember a conversation with a missionary priest at Maryknoll early in 1941. "As an American of Irish descent", he said to me, "I do not need to be reminded of the darker side of British Imperialism, but I often tell my compatriots that there is no empire in which the Catholic Church has, on the whole, been more fairly treated. The Church will have plenty of problems if the Empire packs up." I remembered this prediction when I visited Pakistan and India in 1950. Catholics in Pakistan are unmolested so long as they keep to themselves, but face dangers if they start converting Muslims. The Church is tolerated, but no more. In India there are disquieting symptoms in some states, such as Kerala, where the Communists have gained control, of increasing pressure against the Church. I spent last February lecturing for the British Council in the Lebanon, Persia and

Turkey. Catholics have been leaving Syria and Egypt in increasing numbers as the economic pressure against them increases. The President of the Newman Society to which I gave a talk in Beirut was the son of a Catholic who had to leave Egypt as the result of a camouflaged policy of making things uncomfortable for Catholics. I was in Beirut when the integration of Syria with Egypt was proclaimed, and on my way to lunch with the Maronite Patriarch I passed the first Muslim demonstration in favour of including Lebanon in this new Arab republic. It is still more than doubtful whether the Lebanon, a Christian enclave, can resist a pressure which, as I write, has already produced rebellion and civil strife.

Never has Christendom faced greater perils, and this surely increases the importance of good relations not only between the nations of the free world but also between the different Christian communions. You will find on page 187 of this book a letter which appeared in The Times *during the Spanish Civil War. "Between those", wrote Cardinal Hinsley, "who believe in Christ as true God and true Man and worship Him, there should be charity —the effort to draw nearer to Him and to one another. This means not only friendly relationship, but mutual help in defending the civilization which is founded on the truths enunciated in the Nicene Creed."*

Perilous though the situation be, there is something to set against the loss of whole provinces to the Communists. Since we met in Zermatt last summer I have stayed with friends in Italy, Spain, Belgium and Germany and am encouraged by the clear evidence that in all these countries the position of the Church is more secure than at any time in the last fifty years.

Well, we shall certainly have a great deal to discuss when we meet again in October, by which time this, my fifty-first book, should have been published. It is, so experienced authors assure me, the first fifty books which are the most troublesome.

Till October, then, au revoir.

ARNOLD LUNN

Hotel Edelweiss, Mürren, May 31st, 1958.

CONTENTS

I

RONALD KNOX

On July 13th 1933 Father Ronald Knox, who died on August 25th 1957, received me into the Church, and I had hoped, on the twenty-fifth anniversary of my reception, to have served his Mass, as I had so often done in the past, at The Old Palace, Oxford.

Though we were born in the same year, Knox was a year senior to me at Balliol. He was my predecessor as editor of *The Isis*, the undergraduate weekly, but we moved in very different sets and his recollections of me as an undergraduate were unflattering. "I thought of you", he admitted many years later, "as a sour Dissenter." In point of fact I was never a Dissenter, for I was brought up as an Anglican and considered myself an agnostic when Knox and I first met at Oxford, and my contacts with Knox were, if not cordial, at least faintly friendly. In my Oxford Journal I recorded the fact that I "went as Knox's guest to a paper (read by Knox) at 'The Shaftesbury'. Brilliant paper".

Knox's opinion cannot have been quite so unfavourable as he came to believe for he gave me, as President of the Oxford Union, an official nomination for the Library Committee, the first step towards the secretaryship, the highest office which I held. Knox's triumphant progress to the presidency was never seriously challenged, for as a wit he was famous even as an undergraduate, but it was at the Union that he found himself, perhaps for the first time in his life, committed to the defence of an unpopular decision. The Union had been attacked in the columns of a newly founded periodical for undergraduates, *The Tuesday Review*, and the Committee decided to subscribe to this paper and make it available for reading in the Club rooms. This was intended to damage the sales, for undergraduates who could read the paper at the Union would not buy it in the streets. *The Isis* was not available to members of the Union except in bound copies on the library shelves. It was widely felt that the Union had been a shade petty in indulging in reprisals on an undergraduate paper and when the matter was brought up in private business the Committee were only saved from defeat by a compromise. Knox, who was in the chair, looked uncomfortable. He was ill prepared even for momentary unpopularity but must have been cheered by the readiness of his friends to assume the main burden of the defence.

Knox was received into the Church in September 1917, and he described his conversion in *A Spiritual Aeneid*. The earlier chapters of this book are a record of unbroken success, scholarly and social. He was elected to "Pop", membership of which is confined to the élite of Eton, a term before he would have been officially admitted as Captain of the School. At Balliol he was elected to the Annandale, an exclusive society consisting mainly of Etonians. In later life Knox remarked to me that he was far from proud of *A Spiritual Aeneid*, and the kind of critics who maintain that the literary ability of converts suffers a sharp decline after reception would find no support for this view if they compared *A Spiritual Aeneid* with his later works, *Enthusiasm* for instance. I remember being particularly irritated by a passage in which this spoiled child of fortune, for as such I regarded him, claimed to have an instinctive sympathy for lost causes, the only evidence for which was a sentimental sympathy with the Stuarts. I had entered Harrow just before the Boer War ended. My father, who lived in Harrow, was notorious as a Radical and as a Pro-Boer and I had defended his views with tenacity, and been heartily kicked for my pains. "I have always", wrote Knox, "taken a Catonic pleasure in the defeated." *Sed victa Catoni* . . . no doubt, but there were no Catos at Harrow to endorse and defend my attitude to the defeated Boers. If Knox, I reflected grimly, had been a Pro-Boer at Eton he would have discovered the difference between floating comfortably down and "setting his head against the stream".

In brief, the book exasperated me and I found relief in the catharsis of an essay on *A Spiritual Aeneid*. The next problem was to find a publisher. Nobody would publish the essay as it stood, but what about a book of essays on converts to Catholicism? Such was the genesis of *Roman Converts*, a study of five eminent converts, Newman, Manning, Chesterton (who wrote long and friendly review articles on the book both in *The Illustrated London News* and also in the *Dublin Review*), Ronald Knox and Tyrrell. I spent three years over that book and read widely, for I could not analyse the suasions that induced brilliant men to accept the claims of Rome unless I began by a detailed study of Catholic theology and apologetics. Knox's book provoked me into examining the case for the Church and was thus destined to be the first important influence in directing my steps to the Eternal City.

I sent a copy of the book to Ronald Knox, and was disarmed by his charming reply: "Thank you for the compliment, for it is I suppose a compliment of sorts, like the crocodile pursuing Captain Hook." I remember thinking at the time that there must be unsuspected reserves in that strange religion of his, if he could reply with such humour to so hostile a study of himself and his book.

Many years later, on the day before Father Knox received me into the Church, I remarked to him that if he had written the kind of letter I deserved, I should never have suggested collaborating in the book which had such an influence on my conversion.

"I know", replied Father Knox. "You narrowly escaped receiving the most terrific snorter. I had just drafted it out. Instead, with a real effort I sat down and wrote a reasonably polite reply. This would seem", he added characteristically, "to be one of the few occasions on which doing the right thing has had the right results. It was clearly right not to send you a snorter, and I'm glad that for once doing the right thing did not have disastrous consequences."

But for Knox I should not have written *Roman Converts*, and but for *Roman Converts* I should not have written *The Flight from Reason*, the theme of which was suggested to me by Douglas Jerrold, who had read and enjoyed *Roman Converts*. So once again my reaction to a book which I disliked was the indirect cause of a prolonged study of the Catholic case.

Early in 1930 I reviewed Ronald Knox's *Caliban in Grub Street*. The book delighted me and in the course of a desultory correspondence with Father Knox I broached the suggestion of a joint book to consist of letters in which I should attack and he would defend the Roman claims. It is often suggested that it was this book, *Difficulties*, which transformed me from a bitter enemy of the Church into a convert. This is an oversimplification. I began the book in the year in which *The Flight from Reason* was published, a book which was reviewed by one writer under the impression that I was a Roman Catholic. After this book appeared I was invited to

Stonyhurst and asked, though not a Catholic, to talk to a class in the hour set apart for religious instruction. I was emerging from agnosticism, not Anglicanism, and like most agnostics felt that Catholicism was the only logically defensible form of Christianity. Douglas Woodruff and Father D'Arcy had as great an influence on my conversion as Father Knox and it was not indeed until nearly two years after I wrote my last letter that Father Knox received me into the Church.

Difficulties is one of the favourite books of a sound Protestant, a great friend of mine, Colonel C. A. de Linde. "I cannot understand", he often says, "how you became a Catholic after wiping the floor as you did with Knox." A Catholic, after I had been received, referred to this book and remarked, "The only person who thinks that Knox won is Lunn." More discerning were the comments of Antony, Viscount Knebworth. Antony, who won his half blue as a boxer, had a connoisseur's interest in verbal boxing. "You scored point after point," he said, "but the odd thing is that you did not make the least impression. There is an odd reserve of strength about Knox's letters which is most impressive." After Antony was killed flying his father sent me his copy of *Difficulties* and it was clear to me from the passages which he underlined how deeply he had been impressed by Knox's informal apologetics.

Knox could, I know, have made his letters superficially more effective to the outside public but for the fact that his object was not a striking dialectic victory which might well have provoked me into trying to improve my weapons of offence, but my conversion. He knew that I was pro-Catholic. He suspected that I was reluctant to cross the frontier which separates the pro-Catholic from the Catholic and he feared that I might linger like Mallock indefinitely on the threshold of the Church. Though it is an oversimplification to suggest that his letters were the only important factor in my conversion, there was one sentence which certainly hastened my submission to Rome. "There have been people—Mallock is the obvious instance—whose admiration for the Church seemed to kill in them any appreciation of other religious approaches, yet who never, at least till death was upon them, found their way in. I would not have you undergo that agony of soul." I was touched by the evidence of personal feeling in this reference to Mallock, and for once I felt that Knox was addressing me and not a crowd of unidentified readers.

After exchanging a few of the letters published in this book I had suggested coming up to Oxford to see him, and he had replied that his time was so fully taken up with the undergraduates entrusted to his care that he had little time to spare for non-Catholics. Never did a priest make less apparent effort to win the confidence of a potential convert. Had I been easily snubbed we would not have met, but I persisted and Father Knox allowed me to lunch with him at Oxford, and remarked as I left that if I wanted to come and see him again he would not mind much.

If he treated me with more tenderness in our correspondence than many of his Catholic readers might have wished this was only because he detected the occasional sign of an approaching agreement masked for the moment by increasingly aggressive attack. In a new edition of his book to which we both contributed additional letters, he wrote:

> It [our book] gives you the rare opportunity of seeing a fellow creature snap-shotted in the act of getting the grace of faith. To be sure there is no lack of *récits de conversion* . . . But even in the *Confessions* of

St. Augustine, even in the *Apologia*, you are conscious that your author is reading the past—how could it be otherwise?—with the eyes of the present. But you, writing at the moment when the thing was happening, have preserved the authentic record of a defeat. You were clutching at straws, as we commonly do when we begin drowning in the well of truth; and all the time with less confidence, less hopefully . . . It was a good thing, I think, that you did not choose a more adroit opponent . . . in proportion as the reader is led to exclaim, "Fancy being convinced by arguments like that!" he will be led to wonder whether it is, after all, entirely a matter of argument. *Di me terrent et Jupiter hostis*—you were up against something you hadn't bargained for, and it wasn't me.

A lay apologist defending the Church enjoys a greater freedom than a priest for the same reason that back-benchers are allowed greater freedom than cabinet ministers, whose pronouncements commit the Government. Father Knox's defence of the doctrine of eternal punishment in our book was more conservative than the views which he expressed in private. No Christian, Catholic or Protestant, could repudiate the belief in eternal punishment without repudiating Christ, in whose teaching this belief is central, but Catholics differ widely as to the nature of the punishment. In my controversy with Cyril Joad (*Is Christianity True?*), Joad wrote an eloquent attack on the doctrine of eternal punishment. Though I was not a Catholic at the time I was anxious to defend the doctrine within the limits of Catholic orthodoxy. I submitted what I had written to a distinguished Catholic theologian who said: "Nothing in your letter is contrary to what has been defined *de fide* about hell, but your interpretation of the doctrine would probably be censured if you were a Catholic." An American priest, however, not only endorsed but enthusiastically applauded what I had written. "At Last a Sane View of Hell" was the title of an article which he wrote and published in an ecclesiastical review. I was not surprised when he was censured for the rashness of the views which he was defending. The fact is, of course, that opinions which are regarded as "theologically rash" can be ignored if expressed by a layman but not if expressed by a priest. There was little difference in substance between the views which I expressed in my letter to Joad and the views which I expressed in *Now I See*, but *Now I See* in its Italian translation received an *imprimatur* in Rome, notoriously the most difficult *imprimatur* to get.

Knox was a little uneasy about my orthodoxy so far as hell was concerned and on the eve of my reception he said, "By the way, I've just been reading your letter about hell in our correspondence. I presume you've changed your views since then."

"Of course."

"Well what *do* you believe about hell?"

"I believe all that the Church teaches", I replied firmly.

"But what does the Church teach?"

"Well you ought to know", I said. "You're a theologian."

"I suppose we must pass that", said Knox.

My father, by an odd coincidence, had much the same difficulty when he was being examined for the Methodist Ministry, and his orthodoxy, like mine, was suspect.

"Do you believe", asked the examiner, "in eternal punishment?"

"I believe in eternal punishment of the finally impenitent", answered my father.

"And who, in your opinion, are the finally impenitent?" asked the examiner.

"That is a mystery which I do not profess to solve", said my father.

"I'll admit to you", said Knox after he had given me a pass mark for my answer on hell, "that hell was the only difficulty which I mentioned to the priest when he received me. I believed in hell because it is an integral part of the Christian religion. The doctrine of eternal punishment is like a bulky parcel which I could only just squeeze into an overflowing bag."

"And then only", I said, "because it is a Revelation bag."

"A priest whom I knew", Knox continued, "confided to me that he cherished a hope that our Lady at the Judgment Day would intercede with God and that all souls would be released from hell, but I do not see how one could reconcile such a hope with the explicit statements of our Lord."

I spent many a weekend with Knox at The Old Palace, the home of the Oxford chaplaincy, and I gradually came to see that the letter in which he had tried to put me off coming down to Oxford was not intended as a snub. It was the plain truth that his time was so taken up with his Catholic flock that he had no time to spare for non-Catholics. Certainly no Catholic chaplain could ever have devoted himself with more single-minded determination to the task of reinforcing the faith of undergraduates subjected to the influences of a university environment which is increasingly permeated by secular values. Knox was by temperament a shy recluse but nobody who stayed with him at Oxford would have suspected that he ever found it a strain to live surrounded by undergraduates, four of whom actually lived with him at The Old Palace. I seldom saw him alone in his room. He inspired in the young not only great affection but also great respect and this in spite of an informality—many of his university friends addressed him as "Ronnie"—which shocked his more conservative colleagues.[1] He did not stand on his dignity, but though unexacting as far as deference to himself was concerned he never sought to ingratiate himself by being equally unexacting in his interpretation of Catholic faith and morals. Here is a characteristic extract from a sermon (*Captive Flames*, London, 1940, pp. 5–6):

> And it is such a mistake to think that we ought to try and impress our neighbours by making it clear to them that Catholics are not Puritans, are not strait-laced, are sportsmen like anybody else. The world is very ready to say that of us, but it does not really respect us for it. It does not respect us for being ready to join in rather risky conversation and enjoy rather doubtful jokes; it does not respect us for being careless about what company we keep, and what places of amusement we go to. It respects us if it sees that we shrink from the touch of anything that may defile us; if it sees that the virginity which is practised in the cloister has its complement and its fruit in the chaste conversation of the Catholics who are living in the world.

There is one sentence in *The Mass in Slow Motion* which explains why Knox could get away with the kind

[1] "All my life", he wrote, "I had been indifferent to the use of titles; complete strangers referred to me, sometimes in my hearing, as 'Ronnie Knox'—if anything it was the surname that was regarded as optional." (*On Englishing the Bible*, London, 1949, Preface, p. v.)

of informality which in some preachers might be resented by the young.

> Goodness knows how many times you've watched me turn round and greet you with the *Dominus vobiscum*, or pass from side to side of the sanctuary asking God to keep *this* and *this* and *this* soul safe till it reaches eternal life.

These sermons, published by Sheed and Ward, were delivered to a girls' school, the Convent of the Assumption, which was evacuated in 1940 from Kensington to Aldenham. As you read these sermons you do not merely feel, you *know* that Knox was not trying to impress *himself* but the Church on his congregation. His passionate determination to evoke in his young listeners a love for and understanding of the Mass shines through the transparent veil of what he describes as "a highly specialized art-form, that of sermons to school girls". This book is not only an ideal gift for the young but also for the old. The very unconventionality of this "specialized art-form" helps to fix in the reader's memory things he might otherwise forget. Consider for instance this comment on *et omnium circumstantium*:

> Having been through that bit of self-humiliation, the priest is now allowed to remember that he is a human being, and some people do interest him more than others. He is allowed, for a moment, to stop talking Latin; to think, for a moment, of the people for whose needs he personally wants this Mass to be an availing sacrifice. I ask God to convert Stalin or whatever it may be. And immediately after that I go on to say *et omnium circumstantium*, "Please don't think I want you to listen to *me* more than to any of those horrible

little creatures who are fidgeting behind me. *Quorum tibi fides cognita est, et nota devotio*—they do really believe in you, they are really quite pious, some of them, and each of them has her own intention that she is thinking about at this moment, and it's just as good as mine. So please take it that this goes for Mary Jane's intention as well as mine. *Pro quibus tibi offerimus*; I am offering this sacrifice for them just as much as myself. *Vel qui tibi offerunt*, and they, just as much as myself, are *offering* this Mass, so please don't convert Stalin if you would sooner convert Mary Jane's aunt. They are offering the Mass *pro se suisque omnibus*, for themselves and all they love; their souls want saving, they need health of body and soul, preservation of body and soul from all harm that might befall them; some of them asked rather specially to be called this morning, so please bless every one of them every bit as much as me."

The young are quick to resent patronage and to despise those who attempt to ingratiate themselves by playing down to them and interpolating the kind of slang which they suppose to be current among those whom they are addressing, but a friend of mine who heard these sermons, as a girl, assured me that the girls were enchanted with his humour and that the very unconventionality of his approach impressed on their minds the deeper lessons which he was trying to bring home to them. They responded to the passionate sincerity of his preoccupation with their souls, and instinctively realized that if he seemed sometimes to lower himself to their level it was only to raise them to his or rather to a level far above anything which he, in his humility, believed himself to have attained. "The wittiest churchman in England", as he was described in an admirable *Times* obituary, "was as earnest as he was witty and as devout as he was diverting", with the felicitous result that his wit reinforced rather than detracted from the essential earnestness of his aim. Though he was acutely conscious of his responsibilities for the souls entrusted to his care he did not go out of his way to make converts, "for as a rule", he wrote to me, "no good is done by arguing the Catholic case with an individual unless he has already begun to be attracted to the faith (or unless he asked for it as you did!)."

"The Church", he once remarked to me, "gets on by hook and by crook, the hook of the fisherman who hopes for a rich haul of converts, and the crook of the shepherd whose chief concern is to safeguard his own flock." And he added characteristically, "I'm more of a crook than a hook."

In his attitude to other communions Knox was detached rather than aggressive. I once asked him whether he did not think it needlessly irritating to refer to Anglo-Catholics as Protestants.[1] "I don't refer to *them* as Protestants," he said, "but I'm entitled to say, 'When I was a Protestant.'" Nobody would describe the Greek Orthodox as Protestants and yet like pre-conversion Knox they protested against the claims of the Pope, to which I suppose Knox would have replied that the Tsar, unlike the Head of the English Church, did not at his coronation swear to defend the Protestant religion. My own instinct is to emphasize the points on which we agree with Anglo-Catholics, but when I said something to this effect Knox

[1] In the pages which follow I shall sometimes use the word "Protestant" as a convenient abbreviation for *all* who protest against the claims of Rome. I can hardly be expected to write instead: "Greek Orthodox, Anglo-Catholics, Anglicans who regard themselves as Protestants, Nonconformists . . ." but I should never specifically refer to Anglo-Catholics as Protestants.

replied: "But you were never an Anglo-Catholic, and you were never taken in by Anglo-Catholic claims", and he added, "I have to keep reminding myself that I was in perfectly good faith when I maintained that the Church of England was a branch of the Catholic Church and consequently I must not doubt the good faith of those who continue to believe what I once believed."

I asked him once whether he felt nearer to a Baptist like Dr. Horton, with whom he agreed on the basic Christian doctrines, or an agnostic like Gilbert Murray. "Of course, I'm nearer in belief to Dr. Horton", he replied. "But if you ask me which of the two I'd choose for a companion on a walking tour it would be Gilbert Murray all the time." Knox would have preferred Gilbert Murray not only to Dr. Horton but also to the less congenial members of his own Church. Those who belonged to the household of the Faith were very dear to him, but he would have been honest enough to admit that because of the frailty of our nature our cultural sympathies are often stronger than community of faith. "I'm not going to decide", he wrote to me, "whether the average Catholic or Mexican is what you call 'a better man' than the average Protestant Englishman; I do not know—I know which I would rather take with me on a walking tour, but that is not the same thing. I prefer Englishmen to the natives of any other country in the world, but that is not going to do them much good, poor dears, at the Day of Judgment."

Knox's circle of really intimate friends was very small but there was an outer circle, to which I hope I belonged. In his personal relations with such friends he was too reserved to say anything which might imply a modicum of affection. During the final phase of our *Difficulties* correspondence I was passing through a time of acute financial anxiety for the family firm was threatened with liquidation. "I do hope", said Knox with an unusual touch of tenderness in his voice, "that things will turn out all right", and then, as if embarrassed by the hint of sentiment, he added: "If you do become a Catholic, it would be a pity if this could be explained as the result of a mental breakdown following acute anxiety." I assured him that I would bear this in mind.

Knox found it easier to express sympathy in deed than in word. I remember, the first time I served his Mass, being surprised to discover a cushion on the altar steps. He had guessed that an old mountain injury might make kneeling painful to me, as indeed it sometimes does. He hid from the world, as the writer of *The Times* obituary truly said, "a serenity of spirit born of a humble love of God and a profound compassion for His creatures".

In *A Spiritual Aeneid* he confessed to vanity as "one of the vices I knew to be in my nature", and provided the enemy with evidence in support of this admission, but vanity is not necessarily inconsistent with humility, for praise may be welcome as an antidote to the gloom produced by self-knowledge. There was an authentic humility about Knox which I only began to discover as acquaintanceship evolved into friendship. His humility and absence of pretentiousness disarmed people who might otherwise have been overawed by his reputation. Priests are exacting judges of eminent ecclesiastics and no priest was more popular with the clergy, particularly as a giver of retreats. He and I once spoke from the same platform, and after we had done our stuff we adjourned to a room where a reception was given for the clerics in the neighbourhood. It was delightful to watch Knox's technique for drawing out a young priest who seemed at first rather shy in the presence of this celebrity. His range of pleasures was narrow. He was happiest in the society of the few intimate friends with whom he felt completely at ease.

He enjoyed the exercise of his craft, writing, and in later years delighted not only in translating the Bible but in expounding what he deemed to be the correct principles of translation. It was very appropriate that his last public appearance should be to deliver the Romanes lecture on translation. Among his minor amusements may be mentioned acrostics and composing epigrams in Greek and Latin.

It required an unusual inducement to persuade him to travel. He admitted to me that he had never been to Rome. "I'm a bad sailor," he said, "and the advice given to bad sailors is to keep away from the engines. I followed that advice when I embarked on the barque of Peter."

I remember crossing the Channel with a Yorkshire couple who were making, so they told me, their first visit to the Continent. I found a porter for them, and saw them into their carriage. The porter slammed down the lady's hat box with unnecessary violence. "Isn't that *just* like those French porters", she exclaimed.

"Madam," I demurred, "as this is the first French porter that you have ever seen, isn't it a bit early to generalize?"

Knox had no such innate prejudices against foreigners. It was merely a question of different wavelengths. Like a cat, he was only really happy in familiar surroundings, and, of course, on his travels he missed the expert helpers whom the born helpee always seems, sooner or later, to attract. This distinction between the helper whose vocation it is to help and the helpee who attracts helpers is my own modest contribution to the noble science of psychiatry. Just as there is a feminine streak in all but the most aggressively masculine of men, so most of us have our helper and helpee sides, but pure types are not unknown, Rainer Maria Rilke, for instance, a helpee in whom it would have been impossible to detect the faintest alloy of helpfulness. In his response to people's deepest needs Knox was, as no one knew better than I, a superb and selfless helper, but in more mundane matters he was a helpee, and thus provided the various helpers who looked after him with ample scope for their particular talents. In my own case the dividing line between my helper and helpee sides coincides approximately with the snow-line. Above the snow-line a helper; below a helpee.

After my conversion I persuaded my father to invite a priest to act as chaplain on our Hellenic Cruises, and in 1937 Knox allowed himself to be manoeuvred into acceptance. The real inducement was not the chance of seeing Greece but the fact that his intimate friends Douglas and Mia Woodruff and Daphne Acton were on the cruise.

When helper meets helpee a good time is had by all, but when helpee meets helpee there is a great sense of frustration and wasted talents, as indeed I discovered when I met Knox at the barrier of the Continental platform in Victoria Station. He handed over his tickets to me and said, "You know all about these things." I took them reluctantly.

"Ronnie," I said severely, "you recently wrote a light essay on helpfulness, which you analysed as 40% love of organizing other people's lives, 30% desire for praise, 20% exhibitionism and only 10% pure altruism. I will do what I can to look after you on this cruise provided that it is quite clearly understood that my motives are 95% altruistic."

At that moment I should have been very happy to welcome as a fellow-traveller a born helper whom I had first met on the cross-Channel steamer to Calais. At the time I was still actively associated with the travel firm which my father founded, and which now belongs to other people. I was engrossed in a book when I was recalled to the outer world by a tap on my shoulder.

"Do you propose", asked a brisk and attractive young woman, "to spend the night on this ship? Because if not you had better take note of the fact that we're at Calais. Is this your first visit to the Continent?"

I replied—God help me—that it was. You see, the born helpee is always tempted to exaggerate his helplessness when he has the luck to run into a born helper. The helper collected a porter, took me through the customs, found me a corner seat, and booked me a reservation for the first service in the dining car.

"You know," she remarked as we sat down to dinner, "you ought not to travel alone. You should join one of Lunn's conducted tours. I did once, just to learn the ropes. Of course now I can look after myself."

"You'd make a wonderful conductor", I said. "Have you ever thought of applying for a job with Lunn's?"

"Well, actually my present job comes to an end next spring and I'd love to be one of their foreign representatives next summer, but I don't know anybody in Lunn's."

"I know one of the directors, Arnold Lunn. In fact there is nobody I'm fonder of than Arnold and there is nothing he wouldn't do for me."

"What luck!" she exclaimed. "Will you give me an introduction to Mr. Lunn and tell him how good I am at looking after the helpless?"

So I gave her an introduction to myself and she got the job.

I discovered on this Hellenic Cruise that Knox was not easily moved, at least to articulate enthusiasm, by the beauties either of nature or of art. I was standing with him in the corridor as our train left Lucerne. It was a perfect summer morning and beyond the enchantment of the lake and beyond the green foothills of the Brünig the triple-crested Wetterhorn invaded the blue glory of an Alpine sky. Annoyed by Knox's lack-lustre reactions I exclaimed, "Don't sneer at the Wetterhorn, Ronnie."

"He's not sneering at the Wetterhorn," said Douglas Woodruff, "he's putting up his lorgnettes and asking, 'Do we know the Wetterhorn?'"

Some days later I was standing beside Knox as we sailed up Phaleron Bay. It was a perfect morning. Knox had never been to Greece and I was curious to discover whether the sacred shrines of Hellenism, Athens and the Acropolis, could evoke in him visible enthusiasm, but his reaction to Athens was not noticeably more enthusiastic than to the Wetterhorn. I felt like poor Boswell, who had hoped in vain that something in Scotland would stir Johnson to enthusiasm, and who, when they crossed the Irish Channel and visited the Giants' Causeway, exclaimed with undiminished hopefulness, "Surely, sir, this is worth coming to see?"

"Worth seeing," said Johnson, "but *not* worth coming to see." I quoted this comment to Knox. He smiled. "That's what I feel", he said, "about anything abroad."

"I think", wrote Knox in the extra letter which he contributed to the new post-conversion edition of *Difficulties*, "that I have less stomach now for controversy, and I am surprised at the energy with which I kept up the shuttlecock in those days." It would have been truer to say that his zest for controversy had been deflected from apologetics into arguments about translation. Whereas he replied with disarming gentleness to my attack on *A Spiritual Aeneid*, he wrote me an extremely cross letter when I criticised his translation of the Gospels.

One need not be a scholar to have decided views on biblical translations, for the Bible is for all men. There are Catholics, of whom I am one, who would have preferred, instead of a new translation, an adaptation of the Authorized Version. There is nothing revolutionary in this suggestion, for when Challoner revised the Douai he incorporated great chunks from the Anglican Bible. Unfortunately, whenever he came to a passage whose beauty or whose associations had rendered it familiar to all Protestants his nerve failed him, and he either produced one of his own translations, or altered a word or two, or changed the order of the words, thus ruining the rhythm. Compare, for instance,

> Wherefore if God so clothe the grass of the field, which today is, and tomorrow is cast into the oven, shall he not much more clothe you, O ye of little faith. (Matt. vi. 30, A.V.)

with

> And if the grass of the field, which is today and tomorrow is cast into the oven, God doth so clothe: how much more you, O ye of little faith. (Challoner.)

Instead of adopting the rational principle that one might as well be hanged for a sheep as for a lamb, Challoner stole little worth stealing and seems to have assumed that he might as well be hanged for a lamb as for a sheep.

Now, the Authorized Version is part of the literary heritage of all Englishmen, Catholic, Anglican, Dissenter or agnostic. The index to Ruskin's works, for instance, cites no less than three thousand scriptural quotations without mentioning countless allusions which would be unintelligible to a reader unfamiliar with the Authorized Version. Why should we Catholics create *unnecessary* obstacles between ourselves and other English Christians? Why must we even have different names for so many Biblical characters? What Catholic mother would ever talk about a Noe's Ark to her children? Why not imitate the robust confidence of the early Church, which boldly appropriated anything it required from classical antiquity, building the columns of pagan temples into Christian churches, adapting her own feasts to synchronize with the pagan feasts and incorporating details of pagan ceremonies? The revisers of the New Testament produced one of the worst of modern translations and then wisely adopted the principle of adaptation rather than of retranslating for the Old Testament. Only where the text of the Authorized Version was obviously at fault or unintelligible they substituted a more correct or more intelligible translation and the result is a translation which preserves the noble prose and familiar quotations but which is scholarly and intelligible.

Before the final edition appeared Knox and I had some correspondence about a text (John ii. 4) which Protestants often quote to justify their dislike of what they call Mariolatry. Shortly after I became a Catholic I was crossing the Atlantic and enjoying my book on deck when an American bishop sat down beside me. He knew my father and he hinted that he had read of my conversion with surprise and with regret. I said nothing. I have forgotten the tenor of his subsequent remarks but there was something about the great importance of always reading the original documents instead, so he seemed to imply, of translations doctored to suit the Roman thesis. I offered no comment. "I wonder", he continued, "what you, as an educated convert, make of Mariolatry? Our Lord had no exaggerated reverence for his mother."

"What makes you say that?" I asked.

"Well, you remember how he turned on her at the marriage in Cana and said, 'Woman, what have I to do with thee?'"

"Bishop, I think you have been stressing the importance

of quoting the original documents. Why then quote a translation?"

"I can't remember the Greek", said the Bishop. I could. I have a controversialist's memory, and am therefore often credited with erudition, which I don't possess. I don't suppose I could quote ten verses of the New Testament in the original Greek but as it happened I was able to quote: *τί ἐμοὶ καὶ σοὶ γύναι* of which the literal translation is "What is that to me and to thee, Lady?" Here is the relevant quotation from the Liddell and Scott dictionary: "*γύναι*, vocative, term of respect, mistress, lady."

"Well, anyhow," said the Bishop, "there are many women in history whom I prefer to the Virgin Mary."

It was a hot day, so I evaded further controversy with the conciliatory remark, "There's no point in arguing about questions of taste, but you will forgive me for saying that I prefer God's taste to yours."

In reply to my suggestion that Knox might substitute "lady" for "woman" he wrote, "Only tramps address a woman as 'Lady'." His translation reads, "Nay, woman, why dost thou trouble me with that?" and in a footnote he writes:

> The Greek here is ambiguous; some would interpret it, "What concern is that of mine or of thine?", but it is more probably understood as a Hebrew idiom, "What have I to do with thee?", that is, "Leave me alone, do not interfere with me." "Woman" was an address used in the ancient world without any suggestion of disrespect.

After the New Testament had appeared I wrote an article in which I was rash enough to suggest that once or twice the Authorized Version was not only verbally

I have spent an hour trying to find the letters which Knox and I exchanged about his translation. In my wandering life letters often go astray and those I receive are lost. A letter of mine, which was readdressed four times because on each occasion I had just left the previous address, was returned by the Swiss Post Office to the sender, whose name and address were on the envelope, with a gummed label, *Gestorben*, *Décédé*, *Decesso*. Anybody who gives that much trouble to the Swiss Post Office is officially deemed, in three languages, to be dead.[1] By a strange coincidence, though I did not find the letters for which I was looking I turned up in succession two letters both on the same theme, the first from my daughter-in-law, Antoinette, who wrote, "Nobody seems to know where you are, and when they do you'll be somewhere else", and the second from Knox to my wife. I had apparently written to Knox on a scrap of Ski Club paper (from its old address in Hobart Place) and had forgotten to add the Swiss address from which I was actually writing. "Apart from the pleasure", Knox wrote, "of hearing you like *The Gospel in Slow Motion* I'd be glad to have a chance of getting a letter (enclosed) to Arnold. How is one to find out his lurking places? His last letter is headed '3 Hobart Place, Eaton Square', and he says he writes 'surrounded by Alpine cows'—a most improbable picture."

The first of the letters I was looking for was, as I well remember, a very cross reaction to my criticisms of his translation. I replied by asking him as a priest to give me his opinion on a question of conscience. Should I continue to plead for what I thought was in the best interests of the Church in England, an adapted Authorized Version, knowing full well that I had not the slightest chance of

[1] My safest address is c/o Ski Club of Great Britain, 118 Eaton Square, London, S.W.1.

success, or should I subordinate honesty to affection and write with more enthusiasm of his translation than I felt? Knox replied with a charming letter which ended by the promise to say Mass for me next day. Here, of course, he had the advantage of me, for I could not reciprocate.

He may perhaps have been thinking of his first angry reaction to my criticism in the preface to one of the wittiest and most fascinating, and at the same time one of the least known, of his many books, *On Englishing the Bible*.

> If you question a rendering of mine in the New Testament you come up against a parental instinct hardly less ferocious than that of the mother-bear. I shall smile it off, no doubt, in conversation, but you have lost marks. . . . I get much more angry with people who like me and don't like my Bible, than with people who like my Bible and don't like me.
>
> It is a humiliating reflection, that careful perusal of the holy Scriptures should engender (or perhaps reveal) in one's character this unreasonable streak of touchiness. I can only comfort myself with the thought that, among the canonized saints, none has been more frequently accused of touchiness than St. Jerome.

Enthusiasm was perhaps Knox's masterpiece. A history of the different sects which can be classified as "Enthusiasts" might easily have been all but unreadable, but thanks to Knox's wit and lightness of touch *Enthusiasm* is fascinating. I described my first contact with the book in *Enigma*:

> I adjusted my belt and as the plane took off from New York to Zürich I opened a book-parcel containing

> Monsignor Ronald Knox's *Enthusiasm*, which I read without a break, excepting for meals, until the small hours of the morning, and this in spite of the interruptions of a young Swiss who was anxious to discover whether I had ever heard of myself. "I once met at Mürren the English ski-pioneer, Arnold Lunn. You will certainly have heard of him?" I admitted that we were, in a manner of speaking, connected since Arnold Lunn's wife was the mother of my son. He was so dismayed by this avowal of illicit relations with Arnold Lunn's wife that he did not interrupt me again.

But though *Enthusiasm* is Knox's masterpiece there are many who will agree with me in ranking his sermons far above anything else which he wrote. His sermons are the key to his life. If he was not wholly free from vanity, if discerning praise was always welcome to him, he was none the less essentially humble, for he was humbled by his appreciation of the gulf which separates a devout and self-sacrificing priest from the authentic saint.

The distinction which he draws between modesty and humility is profound.

> For modesty is only the disinclination to hear our own virtues sounded above those of other men; by humility man learns that simply because he is man he is nothing. . . . We can find excuses for ourselves when we do not rival the Saints in their heroic exercise of other virtues, but it is not so with humility. For in proportion as we are less than they, with all the more justice can it be claimed of us that we should be humble.

This quotation is from *Captive Flames*, a volume of sermons which he dedicated to me. Against the *Nihil Obstat* he wrote "almost an understatement", and "Modesty" is his marginal comment on the concluding paragraph of his dedicatory letter, "Such as it is, then, here it is."

Knox's rare visits to London seldom coincided with my intermittent returns to my own country and we met far less often than I wished. I was therefore both startled, flattered and deeply moved by his dedication of *Captive Flames*, which was, I hope, intended to suggest that I was not forgotten, and was numbered among his friends.

My penultimate memory of Ronnie is a happy one. I was one of the guests at a luncheon party to celebrate the publication of his translation of the Bible in one volume, and to honour a great Catholic whom the *Daily Telegraph* was later to describe in an obituary notice as "the greatest English convert to Catholicism since Newman." While we were waiting for lunch to begin I added to the general gaiety of a festive occasion by an absurd mistake. I have known Evelyn Waugh for twenty years and he normally greets me when we meet with ironic friendliness, but he made no welcoming noise when I approached the group in which he was standing. He had grown a moustache since we last met and as he gave no sign of recognition I assumed that he must be Waugh's double. "But for that moustache," I said, "I'd swear you were Evelyn Waugh."

"Everybody tells me I'm like that stinker," replied Waugh, "that's why I grew this moustache. My name is Blennerhasset." By the time Knox rose to speak I had sufficiently recovered from my *faux pas* to enjoy a masterpiece in the true Knoxian manner.

Next time we met was in a London hospital, a few days before his unsuccessful operation for cancer. Douglas and Mia Woodruff had driven me round. He was his gay witty self and such was the infection of his courage that I left full of hope that he would make a complete recovery.

At the beginning of August 1957 I was lunching at the Villa Taranto, my host and friend of many years being Neil McEachern, the creator of the most famous modern garden in Italy. Among his guests was Lord Evans, physician to the Queen. A rumour had reached me that Knox was dead and I asked my host and fellow guests if they knew whether his death had been announced.

"I am sure I should know," said Lord Evans, "because I'm very interested. Your friend was staying with the Prime Minister at 10 Downing Street, and Macmillan, who is very fond of him, asked me if I would come round and have a look at him. The Monsignor was very anxious to give the Romanes lecture at Oxford and Macmillan wanted me to advise as to whether he should. It was obvious to me that Knox was dying, and this being so there was no point in stopping him giving this lecture, which he had set his heart on doing. Knox wanted to know how long I thought he'd live. His literary plans depended on my answer. He wondered whether it was worth while to start on a new book. How long could I give him? I'm often asked that question, but many of those who ask it do not in their heart of hearts want an honest answer. People cling to life so, and most of us are mainly thinking of ourselves. But your friend really wanted the truth. I felt that he was wholly reconciled to death, and that all that interested him was the time-table. Was it worth while to start a new book? I felt that he was detached from this world. The Prime Minister was impressed in much the same way. Of course he was very fond of Knox but it wasn't only the personal tie which affected him. I wrote to Knox afterwards to tell him that the hour I spent with him was one of the most impressive experiences in my life."

After lunch I walked sadly up to the Villa San Remigio where I was staying. Old memories came back to me, memories of strolls with Ronnie through Christ Church Meadows and of the slow-ripening friendship which had its roots in the formal courtesies of controversy in a disappearing tradition. I paused for a few moments on the Upper Terrace where I had said goodbye, just before Italy entered the war, to my beloved hostess, Anglo-Irish by birth and Italian by marriage, and wondered sadly whether we should ever meet again. This terrace, once the setting for the most sorrowful partings and the most joyful of reunions, is now linked in memory with the day when I lost all hope of ever seeing Ronnie again in this world. Whereas in the war a sudden vision of the tranquil beauty of Maggiore would intrude into noisy skies patterned by tracer shells, on that Sunday afternoon even the blue immensities of the lake and the diminuendo of the hills that stooped towards Lombardy could not hold me. I was back again in The Old Palace, that legacy from an Oxford undefiled by the Industrial Revolution, the dark timbers, the stairs bent by the weight of centuries—how one misses such stairs in the New World—the chapel with its odd acoustics so that the cheerful splashing of undergraduates in the bathroom sometimes competed with the sanctus bell, the dining room where the Curé d'Ars beamed benignly across a large beer barrel . . . all this confusion of memories is somehow inextricably associated with memories of Ronnie and with the discovery of that household "where the human spirit has hearth and a roof".

The chapel in which I was received has now been turned into a club room and a lecture room for the Newman Society, and a larger temporary chapel has been built in the garden, an inevitable change which I none the less regret. I never pass down that little passage which once led from the Chaplain's library to the old chapel without a subconscious expectation of seeing Ronnie reappear. . . . *Expectebant eum oculi mei, et non dabatur.* . . .

There are few books with which I would be more reluctant to part than a volume of Ronald Knox's sermons, selected and edited and presented to me by Evelyn Waugh. In a sermon preached in the new chapel Knox summed up with his own inimitable felicity the social and intellectual climate of The Old Palace.

> I cannot pretend that when I myself was chaplain here, The Old Palace was suspected of any exaggerated sympathy with the ardours, the illusions of Youth. It stood here, a gaunt reminder of the past, calculated to chill the aspirations of the visitor, to snub the half-baked modernism of his outlook. My predecessor, Mgr. Barnes, God rest him, was fond of describing the difficulties his correspondents had, when he first took up residence here, in getting his postal address right. "Vey always used to write to me as Monsignor Barnes, ve Old Place." Well it remained something of an Old Place even in my time; I found my typewriter had an odd trick of falling into the same error. An old place, where the aesthete of the late twenties must expect to find an atmosphere of cheerful Philistinism flourishing unreproved; representational art, and bookshelves guiltless of modern poetry; if you wanted to hear about that kind of thing you went round to Campion.[1] An old place, where the near-left political language of the early twenties found no conspicuous echo; you could air progressive doctrine, but if you wanted a sympathetic

[1] Campion Hall is the Jesuit House of Studies; Walton Well Road, the Catholic Workers' College.

hearing you must look for it in Walton Well Road. Sixteen Hundred and Twenty-eight was inscribed legibly over the door-bell; you had the illusion, in those days, that time had stood still.

Ronald Knox, great master of that delicate instrument for the communication of thought, the English language, will speak to us no more, but we may be sure that his intercession for the congregation which meets in The Old Palace will not cease, and I should be very sad if I could not hope that Ronnie, who received me into the Church, will remember my last letter to him when I knew him to be dying, and will continue to help me in my efforts to achieve an undeserved beatitude.

II

CINEMA SUBSTITUTES

I FIRST saw Assisi a few months after Ronnie Knox received me into the Catholic Church. It was mid-March, the tourist season had not begun, and the upper church of St. Francis's Basilica was empty but for two middle-aged Englishwomen and me. I was standing in front of a fresco depicting a miracle of St. Francis, when I heard one of these somewhat dehydrated ladies murmur in a listless tone, "Of course they had not got the cinema and broadcasting, so they had to have miracles to amuse them". That is the kind of remark one must protect against the erosion of time, and as I had no notebook to record this new light on the miraculous I repeated again and again as I wandered up the Rocca d'Assisi the words which it would have been so sad to forget: "Of course they had not got the cinema and broadcasting, so they had to have miracles to amuse them."

It was March 15th 1933, and the Umbrian hills were still crested with snow, a radiant foil to the vibrant green of the young grass in the valley. I am glad that I first saw Assisi in the spring, for the Umbrian hills, like the mountains that keep watch over the plain of Argos, are hot and dusty when summer robs them of winter's legacy of snow. Moreover, the lyrical loveliness of Umbria when Primavera was scattering her largesse of colour in the valley seemed the perfect setting for the shrine of a saint whose genius flowered in the springtime of Christendom.

I had been rereading Spengler's *The Decline of the West*, and I tried to recall the paragraph in which he had paid a memorable tribute to St. Francis of Assisi. Spengler, who had borrowed, without acknowledgement, from Flinders Petrie the conception of a culture cycle, attempted with outstanding success to relate the religion, art, architecture, music and mathematics of the different phases of culture cycles not only in Christian Europe but also in classical Greece, in ancient Egypt and in the Far East. In the springtime of the culture cycle the dominant economy is that of the farm, the village and what Spengler calls the small "culture cities", such as mediaeval Bruges and Nuremburg, the dominant philosophy a dogmatic religion for which men are ready both to die and to kill, and the dominant art an attempt to interpret the supernatural and timeless beauty which is reflected in the temporal loveliness of this world. The culture cycle ends in the winter of civilization, in the great "world-cities" in which faith withers, in which disillusion and nihilism are reflected in an art which has degenerated into stunts, and in which the creative genius of man finds expression no longer in art but in the marvels of applied science, in the cinema and broadcasting and suchlike substitutes for miracles.

As I wandered down from the Rocca d'Assisi to the "little well-ordered city" of Assisi, the passage in which Spengler had cited St. Francis as a typical saint of a cultural springtime came back to me.

> Compassion likewise demands inward greatness of soul, and so it is those selfsame Springtimes that produce the most saintly servants of pity, the Francis of Assisi, the Bernard of Clairvaux, in whom renunciation was a pervading fragrance, to whom self-offering was bliss, whose *caritas* was ethereal, bloodless, timeless, historyless, in whom fear of the universe had dissolved

itself into pure, flawless love, a summit of causal moral of which Late periods are simply no longer capable . . . Let a man be either a hero or a saint. In between lies not wisdom but banality.

There was indeed a lyrical quality about St. Francis which was perhaps more in keeping with the springtime than with the winter of a culture cycle. A modern saint, suspected of preaching to the birds, might be trailed by television sleuths, but it is, of course, only the accidents of sanctity which change with the passing of centuries. It would never have occurred to the Curé d'Ars to preach to birds, and he could certainly never have written anything in the same genre as the *Canticle of the Sun*, but he was as transparent a medium for the supernatural as was St. Francis of Assisi. The genius of St. Francis was translated into gestures and parables which captured the imagination of the world but which might seem theatrical in an age of television; stripping himself naked, for instance, to symbolize his rejection of all that his unworthy father could give him in the way of material wealth, or proclaiming in the style of a troubadour his devotion to the Lady Poverty, his marriage to whom was the theme of art and song. In comparison to the pageantry of those celebrated nuptials the Curé d'Ars' wedding to Miss Poverty might almost seem to have been contracted at a Registry Office, but the Curé's devotion to poverty was no less single-minded than St. Francis'.

I may claim to have made a conscientious attempt to master the relevant literature while I was writing *Roman Converts*. The bibliography at the end of that book only includes books which I had read and reread, and it covers a wide field which includes Catholic theology and apologetics, various histories of the Oxford Movement, the biographies, autobiographies and other writings of the great converts, Newman, Manning, Tyrrell, Chesterton and Ronald Knox, the riddle of whose conversion I was trying to solve; but there is one obvious lacuna in my bibliography. It does not include the title of any book dealing with saints in general, a book, for instance, such as that miniature masterpiece, Father Martindale's *What are Saints?* or any of those modern biographies of saints which were to make a deep impression on me during the final stages of my approach to the Church. Most of my letters to Ronald Knox, in our joint book *Difficulties*, were reasonably well-informed, and did not lay me open to devastating rejoinders, but if I had had a clue to what Catholics mean by "sanctity" I should have produced a more effective statement of a plausible case.

> There is [I wrote] an amazing similarity of outlook between saints of different communions. Striking indeed is the kinship in spirit between saints as widely separated in time and space as St. Augustine and St. Bernard of Clairvaux among Roman Catholics, Launcelot Andrewes and Thomas Wilson, Bishop of Sodor, among Anglicans, and Richard Baxter and John Wesley among the Nonconformists.

To this Father Knox replied,

> A saint is adorned by God with graces out of the common, for this purpose, among others, that he may demonstrate the divine origin of the Catholic Church . . . I wonder if you would agree with me that Tennyson, if he had taken opium for six months on end, could never possibly have written *Kubla Khan*? And yet he was a perfectly workmanlike poet. The quality which Coleridge has and he has not is something

which you cannot define or analyse; you cannot even prove its existence to a person who does not *feel* it. So I would say that among the non-martyr saints who have been canonised within the last few centuries—the martyrs are in a different category, and we have little material for knowing the inside of the older saints—there is a quality, a touch, which you do not find among the holy men of the other Christianities . . . the supernatural touch which distinguishes them from other good people, as a piece of music played by a real genius is different from the same piece of music played by an absolutely faultless performer.

There is, as indeed Father Knox implied, a distinction between the saints who were unofficially canonized by popular acclaim during their lifetimes and the saints whose contemporaries failed to recognize in them "the supernatural touch which distinguished them from other good people".

The cause of Pius IX has recently been introduced. This does not necessarily mean that he will be canonized, or canonized within a foreseeable future, for the cause of one great Pope, Innocent X, as yet unbeatified, was introduced more than two centuries ago, but one can, I hope, without irreverence, believe that even if he be canonized there will still be a difference between Pius IX and the Curé d'Ars. Pius IX was a holy man, singled out by his Creator for the outstanding privilege of being the medium through which two great dogmas of the Church were infallibly proclaimed, but there was no *apparent* evidence in the life which the world knew of that *numinous*, that supernatural quality which the world immediately recognized in St. Francis of Assisi and the Curé d'Ars. No miracles were attributed to his intercession, and his life was not *conspicuous* for those notes of sanctity which—*if* he be canonized—must have characterized the inner life which the world did not know. If Pius IX is ever canonized this will be equivalent to a declaration by the Church that he practised heroic virtue during his lifetime, that he is certainly in heaven and that his intercession may be asked, but the distinction between Pius IX and St. Francis will remain. The latter was, and the former was not, informally canonized by the *vox populi* long before the official and infallible canonization by the Church.

III

THE EVIDENCE OF THINGS UNSEEN

Let us now consider how far the lives of canonized saints provide "evidence of things unseen", how far the supernatural note in their lives defies the attempt of the materialist to explain holiness by biological and psychological factors.

I was brought up to revere the great social reformers who are the glory of Protestantism in England: Wilberforce who fought for the abolition of slavery, Shaftesbury who was responsible for the Factory Acts, Florence Nightingale who revolutionized our hospitals. My criterion of reformers was pragmatic. Unconsciously I judged them by results expressed in terms of social progress. And it never crossed my mind to inquire whether they were consumed by a passionate love for the individual victim of evil conditions, or to trace the connection, if any, between such love of the individual and the love of God. "Practical Christianity", as I understood the term, meant changing man's social environment rather than saving an individual soul.

That there was something supernatural in the love which the saints felt for the least lovable of sinners was an idea which had all the force of novelty and strangeness when I first encountered it in Father Martindale's *What are Saints?* and in the admirable Knox letter from which I have already quoted. It was Father Martindale's little book which first directed my attention to St. Peter

Claver, who worked for years among the slaves, and but for that book I should never have written *A Saint in the Slave Trade*.

The Church needs not only the saint who is consumed by a passionate love for the individual, but also the social reformer who dedicates his life to the improvement of social conditions. St. Peter Claver's immediate predecessor in South America, Father Alfonso de Sandoval, combined compassion for the individual slave with a continuous campaign against the slave trade. Indeed, his book on the infamies of the slave trade is one of our principal sources of information about that evil commerce.

Father Claver, however, was concerned not with the institution of slavery but with the salvation of the individual slave. Wilberforce hated slavery and Claver loved slaves, and it is easier to hate slavery than to love slaves. Most people would certainly find it less of a strain to play an active part in a campaign for the abolition of a social evil than to be prodigal of love to the most wretched of God's creatures. On one occasion Father Claver took into his arms a negro suffering from dysentery and the wretched man covered him with infectious filth. Magdalen de Mendoza, a coloured woman, was so overcome that she fled in panic from the room. Claver rushed after her.

"Magdalen, Magdalen," he exclaimed, "for God's sake come back! Have you forgotten that these men are our brothers, every one of whom has been redeemed by our Lord's own blood?" What indeed could be plainer? One can imagine the ring of astonishment in his voice. Saints are like that. They always act with shattering conviction on the beliefs which other Christians profess. Claver was genuinely at a loss to understand how mere filth and stench could affect the love which a Christian *must* feel for the least lovable of those for whom Christ died. "Can't you understand, Magdalen? These negroes lying in their filth are our *brothers*. Our brothers for whom Christ died." Magdalen may or may not have understood but she was shamed into returning. His amazement struck her like a whip and down the corridors of time we, too, can hear the echoes of his great surprise.

Now the love which inspired St. Francis to embrace a leper and St. Peter Claver to kiss the ulcerous sores of a negro was, in the strictest sense of the term, not natural. It was indeed supernatural, and this supernatural love of the least attractive of God's creatures is one of the notes of sanctity.

Samuel Johnson's comment on people who tried to demonstrate the blessings of poverty is well known. "You will never find people labouring to convince you that you may live happily on a plentiful fortune." I wonder what would have been Johnson's reply if Boswell had piped up, "But, sir, did not our Lord say 'Blessed are the poor?'"

This was indeed a hard saying which has tormented the consciences of Christians ever since. That great wealth is perilous for the soul and poverty a blessing are truths which are an exacting test of faith. The Quakers, who are literalists over texts which can be twisted to mean that war is always wrong, are untroubled by any necessity to be equally literalistic in their interpretation of the many texts which appear to condemn all accumulated wealth. They argue, I am told, that Christ did not forbid the right use of wealth. Perhaps not, but what about the right use of force? Here again Samuel Johnson is very much to the point.

There are other recommendations which I warrant a Quaker will not take literally; as for instance, "From him that would borrow of thee, turn not thou away." Let a man whose credit is bad come to a Quaker and say "Well Sir, lend me a hundred pounds." He'll find him as unwilling as any other man.

The truth is that saints are in love with poverty whereas ordinary Christians are not. In 1811 Father Jean-Marie Vianney, the Curé d'Ars, took possession of his parish.

> His first task [writes Jean Hellé][1] was to take the furniture out of the rectory, give back chairs and tables and armchairs to the gentry who had loaned them, distribute the rest to the poor of the village, and retire for the night to the attic where he lay down on the bare boards with a bundle of wood for his pillow. He contrived almost to forego sleep and food. He neglected himself in illness and got rid of a severe toothache by having the tooth taken out by the blacksmith with a pair of pincers. . . . He never spent a penny on himself, and he distributed to the poor even the money which had been given him to provide his own doctor's fees. He told the physician not to call as he could not pay for the visit.

St. Francis Borgia, who had renounced the power and wealth which was his as Duke of Gandia, and who entered the Society of Jesus after the death of his wife, exhibited in an almost exaggerated degree the virtue of humility and the love of poverty. His diary for the day of his election as General contains the words *dies meae crucis* ("the day of my crucifixion"). His devotion to his Lady Poverty must sometimes have been embarrassing to those whose faith in Providence was slightly less robust

[1] *Miracles*, Burns, Oates and Washbourne, p. 17.

than his own, as for instance when it took the form of resolutions such as this which he notes in his diary, "To distribute the income of the [Roman] College so that the house remains in the more perfect poverty."

In St. Francis' case faith, as Margaret Yeo said, was always justified.

> There had been that occasion in the Vallodolid college when the Rector had come in despair to Francis, to tell him that there was not a farthing in the house and no food but two small stale loaves. "Ring the bell as usual for dinner." The Commissary-General was obeyed. Novices, students and fathers said grace before an empty table. The brother porter answered a knock at the front door. An old man and a young one handed him baskets heavily laden with meat, fish, bread, cheese, wine, fruit and money and left in silence. All sat down to a lavish meal and it was hardly surprising that the messengers were supposed to be angels in disguise. The same thing had happened more than once and now, in Rome, when there was no money nor any apparent likelihood of alms to supply urgent needs, some had always been given in time to avert starvation or debt.[1]

This devotion to our Lady Poverty is worlds removed from the cold acceptance of poverty recommended by the Stoics. Whereas Epictetus recommends us to learn to wish for what has actually happened to us St. Francis did not wait till Fate reduced him to poverty and then acquiesce. No, he renounced the wealth which his father was prepared to offer him and celebrated with rapture his marriage to poverty.

Renunciation of wealth and deliberate acceptance of

[1] *The Greatest of the Borgias*, by Margaret Yeo (Sheed and Ward).

poverty is, of course, no more peculiar to Christianity than monasticism. It corresponds to some basic law of relations between man and the supernatural world, but what is certain is that the nearer man approaches to the pattern of Christ the greater his indifference to wealth. John Wesley, for instance, discovered as a young man that he could live on twenty-eight pounds a year. When his income was four hundred pounds (as it often was from the sale of his books) he still lived on twenty-eight pounds and gave away the balance, and like St. Peter Claver he never failed to register a naïve astonishment that Christians did not practise what Christ preached, "'Lay not up for yourselves treasures upon earth . . .' How do the Christians observe what they profess to receive as a commandment of the Most High God? Not at all! . . . It might as well be still hid in its original Greek, for any notice they take of it. In what Christian city do you find one man of five hundred who makes the least scruple of laying up just as much treasure as he can.' Shortly before he died he made his will. "I have left no money to anyone," he writes, "because I have none."

There is, alas, so much of Christian teaching which "might as well be hid in the original Greek" as far as ordinary Christians like the present writer are concerned. When my eldest grandson was six years old I gave him a shilling. He was sitting next to his sister, Mary, aged four. "Thank you," said David, "but Mary collects money too." Yes, indeed, we are most of us enthusiastic "collectors", but David had to renounce that particular hobby when he entered the novitiate of the Benedictine Order at Downside.

Many years ago I wrote a book about John Wesley which was, incidentally, adopted by the Protestant Book of the Month Club in America. My search for the passages I have just quoted was rendered unnecessarily difficult by the author's laziness in failing to provide an index. *Felix culpa*, however, for I was thereby forced to reread far more than I should otherwise have done, and thus reminded of one other characteristic of holy men whose lives are dedicated without reservation to the service of God. As far as food, drink and, above all, sleep are concerned the ordinary laws of nature do not seem to apply. John Wesley was on the road as an itinerant preacher for more than forty years, during which time he travelled a quarter of a million miles, preached more than forty thousand sermons, crossed the Irish Sea fifty times and wrote more than two hundred books. He averaged twenty miles of travelling per day, almost always on horseback on the rough English roads of the period; sometimes he rode a hundred miles in twenty-four hours. His lungs had been affected by consumption and yet until a few days before his death at eighty-eight he was working at full speed and rising every morning at 4 a.m.

Here is a record of a week's campaign at the age of eighty-four. He started his journey on Sunday at midnight, travelled for nineteen hours. Rose at 4 a.m. on Tuesday for prayer before the first of his sermons—he often preached three times a day—at 2 a.m. on Wednesday, at 3 a.m. on Thursday and 4 a.m. on Friday. After travelling about two hundred and forty miles in eighty hours he "went off with a gentleman to hear a famous musician that plays upon glasses".

If those of our psychiatrists who devote some thought to the study of religion were to investigate what might be called "the biology of holiness" the results might be embarrassing to their more materialistic colleagues. Consider, for instance, the evidence provided by a study of

St. Peter Claver's life. Father Claver's incredible labours were sustained by a daily average of three hours' sleep and—for food—a few pieces of bread and fried potatoes. He never touched meat, fruit or vegetables, and yet never contracted scurvy. He was sensitive to heat but his Mass was always the late Mass at noon, and though he had normally been at work for eight hours before Mass in all the heat of the tropics he never complained of thirst.

The Curé d'Ars averaged *one* hour's sleep in twenty-four, for he retired at midnight and rose again at 1 a.m. He breakfasted on a glass of milk and his only other meal consisted of a few potatoes and occasionally an egg. Holiness is a force as real as electricity, and like electricity can be recognized by certain results even in the material world. "Holiness", as Francis Thompson writes, "not merely energizes, nor merely quickens; one might almost say it prolongs life."

I have taken these words from Francis Thompson's essay "Health and Holiness", and the passage continues as follows:

> By its divine reinforcement of the will and the energies, it wrings from the body the uttermost drop of service; so that, if it can postpone dissolution, it averts age, it secures vital vigour to the last. It prolongs that life of the faculties, without which age is the fore-shadow of the coming eclipse. These men, in whom is the indwelling of the author of life, scarce know the meaning of decrepitude: they are constantly familiar with the suffering, but not the palsy, of mortality. Regard Manning, an unfaltering power, a pauseless energy, till the grave gripped him; yet a "bag of bones". That phrase, the reproach of emaciation, is the gibe flung at the saints; but these "bags of bones" have a

vitality which sleek worldlings might envy. St. Francis of Assisi is a flame of active love to the end, despite his confessed ill-usage of "Brother Ass", despite emaciation, despite ceaseless labour, despite the daily haemorrhage from his stigmata. In all these men you witness the same striking spectacle; in all these men, nay, in all these women. Sex and fragility matter not; these flames burn till the candle is consumed utterly.

There are many other points which one could single out as characteristic of sanctity. As, for instance, to quote once again from Knox's letter,

> . . . the notion of vicarious suffering for others, as when St. Ignatius stood in the frozen river to save the libertine; a great simplicity, almost childishness, as when St. John Cantius ran after the highwaymen to tell them that he had some money after all; a deliberate foolishness, like that of St. Philip Neri changing hats with other people to make passers-by laugh at him; a fantastic reliance on Providence, like Don Bosco's; a desire to run away, even from a vocation which meant untold good to others, such as that evinced by the Curé d'Ars, and so on. It is quite certain that the ordinary Protestant reader would not be edified by such traits; and indeed some of them are traits which nobody would admire in a man who was not a saint. But, for the sympathetic reader, they show up the medium used for the drawing, which is, I suppose, a completely supernaturalized and, if you will, otherworldly atmosphere. And it is not so much the miracles of the saints which impress me as the fact that, when you read the lives of such people, the miracles seem quite in keeping, quite in the picture; whereas in the biography of any ordinary religious

leader—say Bossuet—they would somehow be out of the picture.

I have shown that one of the notes of holiness can be discerned in John Wesley, and other points singled out as characteristic of sanctity are found in mystics of other religions than the Christian.

Let me anticipate a protest from such Protestants as may read this book. "All the important characteristics of sanctity", they may urge, "are to be found in holy men irrespective of their religious affiliations." Others of my readers may claim that all mystics, whether Christian or non-Christian, belong to the same family. My own conviction that the differences between Christian and non-Christian mystics were as important as the points of resemblance was confirmed when I read Bergson's *Les Deux Sources de la morale et de la religion.* Be that as it may, it is not this or that note of sanctity which seems to me to differentiate saints such as the Curé d'Ars from other holy men, including, be it noted, some canonized saints in the Catholic calendar, but the combination of many such notes in one particular man.

Whether the saints "demonstrate", as Father Knox claimed, "the divine origins of the Church", is a point on which Catholics and Protestants must necessarily agree to differ, but we can at least agree that they provide in their lives overwhelming "evidence of things unseen", and this is a fact of great importance in the struggle against materialism, a struggle in which all Christians should, as Cardinal Hinsley insisted, present a united front. It may well be that had I been a practising Anglican when I read the lives of the Curé d'Ars and other saints mentioned in this chapter, the effect of my researches might have been restricted to the reinforcement of my faith in the supernatural. Emerging as I was from agnosticism, however, the saints had a decisive influence on my conversion to Catholicism, an influence which I tried to sum up in one of my letters to Dr. G. G. Coulton.[1]

> Sanctity [I wrote] is heroic virtue, holiness transmuted by something which is not of this world, goodness which bears the unmistakable imprint of the supernatural. The saint is the final argument for the Catholic Church, for in the Catholic climate sanctity still flowers and still sweetens this tormented world with the fragrance of heaven and the scent of Paradise.

[1] *Is the Catholic Church Anti-Social?*, pp. 225–6.

IV

UNSYNCHRONIZED CATHOLICISM

I RECENTLY read a graphic description by a journalist of the desperate adventures of those submarine hunters who photograph at close quarters and kill or are killed by sharks and barracudas and other unpleasant denizens of the vast deep. I was impressed by the imaginative power with which the writer evoked emotions which he himself had never experienced, but I did not credit him with the courage of the submarine hunters whom he had interviewed, and it would be equally absurd necessarily to credit a man who writes with conviction about saints with anything more edifying than a profound reverence for those whose spiritual dimension is as remote from the dimension in which most of us live as is the submarine world from that surface of the sea in which ordinary folk disport themselves without danger.

This disclaimer is addressed only to those of my readers who have not met me: those who have need no such warning. Witness the following illuminating story of the disillusioned fan with whom I spent a fortnight on a ship in which we were sailing for South America. I had taken the clipper from Lisbon to New York, landed a few days before Pearl Harbour, and left ten days later for Peru. I shared a table with a very likeable priest who evoked not only my affection but also a very genuine respect. Admittedly, his verdict on my own country was less favourable than my own, and this was not surprising, for he was born of Bavarian parents in Bavaria and had left Germany before the First World War. He was not only a loyal but an enthusiastically loyal American, and a wholehearted supporter of the war once it was declared, but he could not help cherishing a deep grudge against the British for what he deemed to be the Machiavellian cunning with which they had, for the second time, manœuvred the country of his adoption into war against the country of his birth. He was convinced that Roosevelt and the British between them would have transformed America into a belligerent even if the Japanese had not done the job for them.

I served his Mass every morning and we had two subjects for discussion; the Church, on which we agreed, and the British, on which our harmony was ruffled by occasional protests from A. L.

At Christmas midnight Mass he preached on our duty to love our enemies. "That was a fine sermon of yours, Father," I remarked, "and perhaps you would follow it up next Sunday by a sermon on your duty to love your allies, a more exacting test of your Christian principles."

As we sailed through the Caribbean Sea I told him that I was very sorry we were not calling at Cartagena because I had a great devotion to St. Peter Claver and would have loved to have seen his tomb.

"Oh, if you've a devotion to St. Peter Claver," said my friend, "there's a book about him which you should read. I've forgotten the name of the author but I thought it a swell book. Let's see, what was it called?" He hesitated.

"Was it by any chance called *A Saint in the Slave Trade?*"

"Yes, that's it," said the priest. "You should read it." And he added sternly, "It would do *you* good."

"I dare say it would," I said sadly, "if I didn't know

the author. And anyhow, I believe in the division of labour. I wrote that book and you can jolly well read it."

"Good heavens," he said, "you wrote it! That's funny." But he obviously did not think it as funny as all that. He was disconcerted to discover that any man who could write with such conviction about sanctity could be so lacking in spirituality. I have, of course, learned by experience that my only hope of retaining the respect of those who like my writings about the Faith is to insist that they remain pen-friends. Any slight influence which I might hope to exercise through my writings is promptly counteracted by my personal example. A case in point was the unfortunate result of a great build-up which I had received from a Catholic hostess with whom I stayed in America and who had done her best to impress her small children with the alleged merits of my work as a Catholic apologist. During my stay the small son of my hostess poked his head round the door and studied with interest my room which I had, as is my habit, transformed if not into a home from home, at least into a sty from sty. He would seem to have done his best to reproduce in his own room the somewhat chaotic effect of mine and when his mother remonstrated he said: "When I grow up I'm going to be just like Arnold Lunn and throw *all* my clothes on the floor."

Though Father Knox's letter about sanctity was one of the more important of the influences which speeded up my conversion, if the Church had consisted mainly of saints and very holy people it would have been as ridiculous for me to seek membership of so select a society as it would be for a man who suffered from acute vertigo to seek to qualify for the Alpine Club. I was attracted to the Church not only by the saints but also by the power of the Church to evoke the passionate loyalty of sinners, and to retain the allegiance of the naturally irreligious.

It was an Anglican friend of mine, whom we may call Anne, who put into words what I now regard as a note of the Church, almost as impressive as the note of sanctity; the power of the Church to retain the allegiance of those whom Anne calls the "naturally irreligious". Anne was a devout Anglican, one of those whose inner life is formed by an unfailing sense of the presence of God in prayer. Her husband, Paul, one of my closer friends, is a history don. He dropped his religion at school, and did not resume the practice of religion until he became a Catholic in his late forties. If there be such a thing as a purely intellectual conversion then Paul's was a case in point. He became a Catholic because he found himself unable to resist the conclusion that of all attempts to interpret history, the Catholic interpretation alone makes sense. He fulfils his obligations and would never dream of missing Mass on Sundays, but I don't suppose he has ever acquired a rosary or attended a retreat. As Paul, before he became a Catholic, had no religion to pass on to his only child, a daughter, and as he had left her religious training entirely to his wife, he felt that it would be unfair to insist on sending Joan to a Catholic school, and not only unfair but unwise, for Joan was devoted to her mother and would have started with an immense prejudice against the Church if sent against her mother's will to a school of which her mother disapproved. The final decision to send Joan to Roehampton was not his but Anne's.

"I expect you were very surprised", said Anne when she and I sat next to each other at a dinner party, "to hear that we're sending Joan to Roehampton?"

"It's very good of you," I murmured.

"Not at all; I'm not doing this to please Paul. If I were certain that my Church would mean as much to Joan as it does to me I wouldn't dream of sending her to a Catholic school, and if she leaves Roehampton a convinced Anglican I'll take off my hat to her. But the fact is that she's not naturally religious. She takes after her father, excepting that she hasn't got his brains. If we sent her to an Anglican school she would probably end up a nominal Anglican—you know, Communion at Easter and Christmas—and I'm not prepared to take that risk. My Church has little hold on the young unless they are really keen on religion, whereas most of your young Catholics seem to go to Mass every Sunday whether they are keen or not. Your Church seems to have some sort of mysterious control even on slack Catholics which is important now that chaperones have gone out of fashion and young girls are much less protected than they were."

"I agree, but don't expect too much from the Church if Joan does become a Catholic. A Portuguese priest who was translating Father Martindale's *The Difficult Commandment* said with a laugh, 'In Portugal the booklet should be called *The Impossible Commandment*'."

"In Portugal, perhaps," said Anne with a slightly disdainful sniff.

"Have you ever been to Portugal?" I asked.

"All the same," said Anne, ignoring my question, "I'm quite sure that your Church is a more restraining influence on young people who aren't particularly devout than ours. It's the ideal Church for the naturally irreligious."

"I would hardly describe that as a fulsome compliment."

"You know what I mean," said Anne firmly, "so don't start trotting out your Catholic saints. What I mean is that you Catholics have an *esprit de corps* which helps to keep people who aren't naturally religious loyal to your Church. It's a bit like my father's feeling for his regiment."

I was glad to recall Anne's comparison between Catholic and regimental *esprit de corps* when a friend of mine, whom we will call Oliver, consulted me about a Catholic nephew of his. Oliver is a prosperous and distinguished doctor. His sister married into one of the oldest Catholic families in the country. Her husband was killed in the First World War, since when she kept house for Oliver, who was a childless widower. Oliver's nephew, her son Dick, went from Downside into the Irish Guards. He is an extremely attractive young man and does not always find it easy to resist those whom he attracts. His uncle and mother had been worried about a siren who had succeeded in having an affair with him but who had failed to lure him into marriage. That episode had just come to an end when I saw Oliver.

"What puzzles me about Dick," said Oliver, "is that he's so fussy about going to Mass. Nothing would induce him to miss Mass. Does he really suppose that it's a greater sin to cut Mass than to have an affair with a siren like that adventuress who hoped to marry him? It seems to me hypocritical to turn up at Mass every Sunday and break the rules about sex during the rest of the week."

"Why hypocritical?"

"Oh, because it's staking a claim to be religious when you're not behaving religiously."

"It doesn't strike a Catholic that way. We don't cease to believe when we cease to behave. If the Communists seized control in England Dick would cheerfully die in defence of the Church."

"Then why doesn't he live for the Church? Why doesn't he keep the rules about sex?"

"Because they're infernally difficult to keep. On the other hand the obligation to attend Mass is easy to observe. You seem to think that because a Catholic can't keep all the commandments he should, to prove his consistency, keep none of them. I dare say Dick hopes that God will make allowances for those who lack the heroic virtue which alone enables a young and very attractive man to avoid the sins of the flesh, but only a slight effort is needed to attend Mass. To cut Mass is like cutting an important parade. It's bad manners, and as good manners are far easier to acquire than good morals, bad manners are in some ways more inexcusable."

"And, of course," said Oliver, "my nephew knows that he can square the Almighty every time he sins by going to confession and getting absolved."

"Dick also knows that absolution does not wipe out the punishment for sin which is at present due to him in purgatory, and also that the absolution is only valid if there is 'a firm purpose of amendment'."

"Many Catholics", said Oliver, "seem to be fairly regular in their relapses."

"Maybe. The Sacrament of Penance is a medicine which does not produce an instantaneous cure. You're a doctor. I hope that your patients are in general the better for the medicines you prescribe, but one dose seldom does the trick, does it? Anyhow, to come back to your first point, Dick's presence at Mass would never be interpreted by Catholics as implying any claim to be keeping the difficult commandment, and in this country, where Catholics are in a minority, there is a very strong Catholic *esprit de corps* which helps to ensure our attendance at Mass even when we are living in sin."

Oliver looked thoughtful. It was clear that he was not arguing for the sake of taking a crack at Catholics. He had no particular prejudice for or against Catholics. He was genuinely seeking for an explanation of something which had puzzled him.

"I'm glad we've had this talk", he said. "It's made Dick's behaviour comprehensible. That point about the *esprit de corps* had never occurred to me."

The Catholic *esprit de corps* is always strongest where Catholics are in a minority as in England. The influence of a Protestant culture on a Catholic minority is discernible not only in reinforcing Catholic *esprit de corps* but in the subtle differences between the atmosphere of the Catholic Church in England and, say, in Italy. Matthew Arnold was struck in his travels by the contrast between the respectability of the average congregation in an Anglican church and the predominance of the poor in Catholic churches. Nothing indeed is so Catholic in its atmosphere as an Italian church in some poverty-stricken village, the kind of church of which Heine may have been thinking when he coined the phrase *grossartiger Schmutz* ("great-hearted dirt"). In such churches, where notices urge the faithful to refrain from spitting out of respect for the house of God, those who with difficulty refrain from spitting in church are as welcome as those who never spit even at home. Moreover the sinner is as much at ease as the saint, the philistine as the aesthete.

I remember escorting an art critic to the Frari in Venice. He went into ecstasies over Titian's "Assumption" over the high altar and rippled into refined shudders when we turned a corner to discover a very different interpretation of our Lady, a gaudy and overdressed doll before which a Venetian peasant was saying her prayers with great devotion. But a church is not a museum; there must be something for all tastes, including bad taste, and in Italy although bad taste (provided that it is indigenous and not imported) knows beauty and elects to pass it by, as E. M. Forster somewhere says, "it attains to beauty's confidence".

I am writing these lines in a room overlooking the bay

of La Mortola. It is Sunday, and at Mass this morning the congregation received the usual reinforcements as the Mass proceeded, the last arrivals neatly timing their entry just as the preacher brought his sermon to an end. Punctuality is the politeness of Protestants. A Protestant who is late for Matins feels very uncomfortable as he tiptoes up the aisle. To be deliberately late for Mass is at least a venial sin but even so I have been long enough in Italy to be shocked when a priest in a small church at home stopped in his sermon to reprove a late comer, a solecism of which no Italian priest would be guilty. An Italian friend of mine once informed me that what she called the "good Mass" began at 11.30 and by this she meant that if one arrived at 11.30 one would fulfil one's obligation, for one would arrive just before the sermon was completed and the chalice uncovered.

I quoted this example of the genial Catholicism of Italy to Paula Sella, the daughter of my hostess, and to her friend Constanza Serralunga, both of whom had spent some time at Oxford.

"But your Catholicism in England is not really quite the same as ours", said Constanza: "It is so *synchronized*."

"Synchronized?" I asked: "What does that mean?"

"Oh well, when I went to Mass in Oxford if I did not kneel when everybody else knelt, or if I knelt when they were not kneeling, sometimes I got unsympathetic looks from those around me. In Italy we are not at all synchronized."

I knew exactly what she meant.

"Well, we too have our unsynchronized Catholics," I replied. "Hilaire Belloc, for instance. Of course he was a Latin, half-French. There is a story about him which every English Catholic knows but which might be new to you. He was standing bolt upright when the synchronized congregation were kneeling down, and a verger who took him for a Protestant who did not know the form tapped him on the shoulder and said, "Excuse me, sir, you ought to kneel at this point." "Go to Hell", replied Belloc. "Sorry, sir", said the verger, "I didn't know you were a Catholic."

Now Hilaire Belloc, as his daughter Eleanor Jebb remarks in her charming memoir[1] of her father, was no saint, and Frank Sheed, if I remember aright, made the same point when he remarked in an obituary notice that the rules for canonization would have to be revised before the cause of Hilaire Belloc could be introduced. It was partly because he was not a saint that he had such an influence on my own conversion. Indeed, for reasons which will I hope emerge in the next chapter, no Catholic writer had a greater influence on my conversion than the unsynchronized Hilaire Belloc.

[1] *Testimony to Hilaire Belloc*, by Eleanor and Reginald Jebb, Methuen & Co., 1956.

V

MEMORIES OF HILAIRE BELLOC

It was as an undergraduate that I first discovered Hilaire Belloc. I picked up a volume of his poems in Blackwell's book shop, was fascinated by what I read and bought the book. That same evening a friend of mine and I dined at the Clarendon. We dined well. Over the port we took it in turns to read and declaim Belloc's poems, and the effect of poetry and port was exhilarating. We were particularly pleased with the poem which began:

Remote and ineffectual Don
That dared attack my Chesterton

and continued through a crescendo of decasyllabic invective:

Don to thine own damnation quoted
Perplexed to find thy trivial name
Reared in my verse to lasting shame.

After we had read this poem to each other more than once it occurred to me that the poem should be recited without further delay to a don in my own college, Balliol, who had spoken disparagingly of Chesterton and who might, for all I knew, be the don who had provoked Belloc. I therefore returned to Balliol and serenaded the don under his windows, and it might have been better for me had he been "remote and ineffectual". So far from being remote he was very much on the spot. Somewhat chastened by our interview, I wrote to Belloc next day to describe the effect of his poetry. Belloc replied on 12th December 1910, from King's Land, Horsham.

> My dear Sir,
>
> This is as it should be and warms my heart! Verse is intended to produce that sort of effect—notably in Balliol, when, in my time, we read and wrote it continually, and, when it seemed insufficient, added music to it, and when that failed, drink. A thousand thanks therefore . . . Whoever the Don is who thinks Chesterton ignorant you can tell him that, in my time. . . .

And here followed a collection of howlers perpetrated by dons, as for instance, "A Don (the Master of his College) asked Maurice Baring 'in what language Russian authors wrote their books'" . . . "Some Dons thought that Tacitus was written by Poggio" . . . "All Dons thought that Homer was written by a committee of Dons" . . . "Most Dons doubt the existence of God", and so forth to the Bellocian climax: "But several Dons killed themselves, which was not so ignorant after all."

Either before or after this exchange of letters I had read and been fascinated by *The Path to Rome*, which remains to this day my favourite book. I reread it every year; Belloc's aggressive Catholicism in this, as in his other books, alternately irritated and attracted me. I was at first bewildered by his rationalism, by his reiterated insistence on reason as the secure foundation of the Catholic faith. As an agnostic with an Anglican background I had always assumed that the Catholics appealed from reason to faith, and it was Belloc's emphasis on reason which encouraged me to investigate the case for the Church, if only to discover whether Belloc's insistence on reason was a private whimsy of his own or orthodox Catholicism. One of the results of this investigation was a book of mine published many years later, shortly before I became a Catholic, *The Flight from Reason*, which was rewarded by a letter from Belloc to the effect that he liked the book so much that he had bought twelve copies to give away to his friends. No letter from a reader has given me greater pleasure.

It was about this time that Douglas Woodruff asked him whether he thought that I would end up in the Church. "Oh, he'll come in all right", replied Belloc.

We first met when I was still at Oxford. Belloc treated younger men, until he knew them well, with a formal courtesy which was rather attractive. He talked about the curious illusion of so many who describe themselves as "rationalists" that their beliefs are anchored in reason, rather than in an uncritical faith in the dogma that miracles do not occur. I told him how much I loved *The Path to Rome*, and he said something to the effect that he had sold the copyright for a ridiculously small sum.

Most of my adult life has been spent out of England and my opportunities for meeting Hilaire Belloc were very limited, but we exchanged letters from time to time, usually on some subject connected with the Church but once on a proposal which he wanted me to lay before my father, Sir Henry Lunn, a well known travel agent. He was anxious to persuade my father to organise a tour to some of the less known but interesting parts of North Africa. I forget the details, and to be honest neither my father nor I took the proposals seriously. Travel agents cater in the main for the untravelled who are nervous of venturing abroad alone, and who are unattracted by "off the beaten track" itineraries. Those whose holidays are limited rightly give priority to the beaten track, to Rome, Florence and Venice rather than to the remoter shrines, and those who have the leisure, the experience and the imagination to seek out hidden wonders are allergic to conducted parties.

My father was delighted to see Belloc not because he was interested in his proposals but because he was interested in Belloc. Belloc assumed that my father was an astute man of business—had this assumption been correct the travel agency which my father founded would still be owned by the family—and that he would have to keep his wits about him to prevent his name and his talents being exploited. His manner was aggressive and he seemed bewildered by my father's attempts to steer the talk away from business into other channels. I was embarrassed, for I knew that Belloc's suggestions were impracticable and that what my father wanted was to meet Belloc, whom he had seen from time to time in the Reform Club. As Belloc rose to go my father thanked him for calling and promised to let him know if he could make use of his interesting proposals. And that was the end of it. Or not quite the end, because I conveyed to Belloc an invitation to lecture on my father's Hellenic cruises, in return for a free cruise, but he was unwilling or unable to accept the invitation.

The great disappointment of Belloc's life was his failure to get a fellowship at Oxford. During the Second World War my brother, Hugh Kingsmill, and Hesketh Pearson visited Belloc at King's Land and described the interview in their joint book, *Talking of Dick Whittington.* My brother asked him why they didn't give him a fellowship at Balliol. "That was out of the question", said Belloc. "Jowett looked on Catholicism as a sect. Harold Fisher wanted to get me a fellowship at New College, but the dons were frightened. They did not know what I'd do. I might come into the Common Room with a girl over my shoulder."

Belloc was anything but a militant Catholic at Oxford. He had indeed, in his own words, "to return to the Faith". His own explanation of his failure—"the dons were frightened"—is I am sure correct. A man who is as contemptuous as was Belloc of academic convention has no grievance if he is denied academic recognition.

H. A. L. Fisher, the Warden of New College, though an atheist—a fact which only became known after his death—entertained feelings of amused though genuine admiration for Belloc. We met one summer at Maloja and I asked him what he thought of Belloc. "I've read all his biographies and historical studies," said Fisher, "and of course I would not trust a single fact in his books unless I had independently verified it, but I have never read a book of his which does not give me some new, stimulating and discerning slant on history. Here's a story about him which may amuse you. On a boiling July day I went into the National Library in Paris and there I saw Belloc standing behind a table on which perspiring assistants were piling up books and pamphlets. Belloc was just getting to work on his biography of Marie Antoinette. He stood there with a smug satisfied expression as if to say, 'These damned dons accuse me of neglecting research. Well, look at this tableful of books.' I took Belloc and the Director of the Library out to lunch and by the time Belloc had got outside of a bottle of Burgundy, he began to develop his ideas about the writing of history. 'History', said Belloc, 'is a matter of flair rather than of facts. You saw all those books which your staff were collecting for me this morning?' 'I did indeed', said the Librarian who had himself spent an hour hunting for them. 'I have a flair,' said Belloc, 'that not one of them contains a single fact which is of the least use to me. I shall not return to the library.'"

This was, of course, largely a stunt. It is clear from Mr. Speaight's valuable biography that Belloc was often an extremely conscientious researcher who would go to immense trouble to get his facts right on points which really interested him. Whereas other historians advertised their researches by copious footnotes, Belloc preferred to conceal his. "Contrary to hostile legend," writes Robert Speaight, "he was (at least in early days) most punctilious in verifying his facts . . . An impression was created that Belloc was much less erudite than in fact he was, and it was an impression that Belloc did a good deal to encourage", perhaps because he enjoyed shocking the academic mind.

I remember a dinner of some society at Oxford at which Belloc was the guest of honour. "You Englishmen talk about civil wars, but you have not the least idea of a real civil war. What were the casualties in the paltry affair between the Cavaliers and the Roundheads? Fifty men killed at Abingdon!" After the dinner I heard a don rebuking Belloc. "My dear Belloc," he said, "how could you possibly say that the total casualties in the Civil War were 'fifty men killed at Abingdon'?" "Did I really say that?" exclaimed Belloc. "What fun!"

Socially Belloc was a man of extremes. Nobody could be more courteous or show a more delicate consideration for the susceptibilities of friends who were not of his Faith, but when he misbehaved his social misdemeanours were on the grand scale. Of this aspect of Hilaire Belloc, Robert Speaight mentions one or two examples in his biography, and here is one of which I was an embarrassed witness. A distinguished American priest, of Irish ancestry, was being entertained by a group of Catholics in London. The priest in question was neither an Anglophobe nor an Anglophile, but on this occasion he was anxious to reciprocate the friendly feeling of his hosts, and the theme of his speech was therefore all that his country and ours had in common as, for instance, a tradition of liberty going back to the Magna Charta. His interpretation of our history was very different from Belloc's, but the occasion called for a tribute to America in general and to our guest of honour in particular. However, Belloc spoke as if he was taking part in a rather cantankerous debate on the Whig interpretation of history, a debate in which our guest and Belloc were on opposite sides. The only thing, he insisted, that English and American Catholics had in common was the Mass.

Our guest, who was one of the most influential Catholic journalists in America, was justifiably incensed. He would in any case have been an advocate of isolationism when the war came, as it did two years later, but the rankling memory of that luncheon could hardly have modified any of his inherited prejudices against England.

During the War I spent a week-end at King's Land, where Belloc was then living with his daughter, Eleanor Jebb, and her husband. He was only in his early seventies but his mind kept returning to the past, particularly to the fellowship he had failed to obtain. Like most anti-Semites, Belloc resented what he deemed the injustice of being accused of anti-Semite sentiments. In the interview which he gave to Kingsmill and Pearson he disclaimed, as he did to me, anti-Semitism. "It was the Dreyfus case", said Belloc, "that opened my eyes to the Jewish question. I'm not an anti-Semite. I love 'em, poor dears. Get on very well with them. My best secretary was a Jewess. Poor darlings—it must be terrible to be born with the knowledge that you belong to the enemies of the human race."

KINGSMILL: "Why are the Jews the enemies of the human race?"
HILAIRE BELLOC: "The Crucifixion."
KINGSMILL: "I see."

He insisted to Pearson that he only wrote for money.

BELLOC: "I hate writing. I wouldn't have written a word if I could have helped it. I only wrote for money. *The Path to Rome* is the only book I ever wrote for love."

PEARSON: "Didn't you write *The Four Men* for love?"
BELLOC: "No. Money."
PEARSON: "*The Cruise of the Nona*?"
BELLOC: "Money."

My visit to King's Land coincided with the Little Blitz of 1944 and the peace of Sussex was doubly welcome after the noisy pother of the London skies. It was therefore with a certain sense of grievance that I heard a German 'plane unloading as it fled from its pursuers. A stick of six bombs fell uncomfortably close with a curiously enlivening effect on the old gunner. He leaped to his feet and lumbered through the door, and seemed disappointed that there was no further sign of action in the sky—for the 'plane had long since disappeared.

At the beginning of the War he had been heard categorically to insist that the Catholic culture of France would be more than a match for the Protestant Prussians, and he never wholly recovered from the collapse of France in 1940. It was to Valmy and to the great Napoleonic campaigns that his mind preferred to return. "The French", he said to me, "have a great military tradition, whereas the English have none." This ruffled my composure. "Perhaps", I said, "it may be an advantage not to have a military tradition, because when we fought the French in Europe, in Canada or in India, we, the unmilitary British, always won. Admittedly we were beaten when the French were led by St. Joan, but whether this was because the French have a military tradition or because they enjoyed the unfair advantage of supernatural assistance, is not clear." The Irish half of me felt slightly ashamed of the emergence of this militant John Bull, for I love France and believe that France is still the lynch pin of Europe, and would not seriously attempt to belittle her military glories, but this was one of the cases where Belloc's exaggerations damaged the cause which he defended. More often, however, his overstatements had a delayed-action effect which was persuasive. The great blasts which he blew on his Catholic trumpet had an erosive influence on the walls of my Protestant Jericho. Though irritated, I was stimulated to read up the subject in order to refute him. I was amused rather than annoyed by his notorious "Europe is the Faith and the Faith is Europe", but I remember very well the dawning suspicion that Belloc's "Europe must return to the Faith or perish" might yet be vindicated by disasters which still seemed comfortably remote. In his famous controversy with H. G. Wells all my sympathies were with Belloc, though I was still an agnostic. Even then I knew that Wells, with his "Existence impresses me as a perpetual dawn", had far less claim to be considered a prophet than Belloc, who replied that Wells's "dawn" was nothing more than the "shoddy remnant of the Christian hope, and when it is gone there will return to us, not the simple paganism of a sad world, but sheer darkness; and strange things in the dark". On which Mr. Speaight justly remarks: "Wells and Belloc both lived to see them; and they were strange indeed."

Belloc was by no means neglected. Even those who detested his militant Catholicism recognised his versatile genius. His *Modern Travellers* and *The Bad Child's Book of Beasts*, which might almost be described as a new genre of humour, enchanted those who were equally allergic to his religion and to his politics. It is therefore all the more surprising that Belloc received hardly any recognition for the one branch of literature in which he was unrivalled by any author.

No writer ancient or modern was his equal as a word-painter of scenery. Whether he was describing the Alps or Norfolk Broads, the sea or the Sahara, he never failed to find the phrase to describe or the metaphor to suggest what *differentiated* the particular mountain or lake, sunrise or sunset, which he was describing, from other mountains, lakes, sunrises or sunsets. The writer who confines himself to factual epithets can only suggest the crude contrasts between, say, the Matterhorn and the Rigi, the Atlantic in a gale and the Mediterranean on a cloudless summer day. Even a generalized word picture may be beautiful, as for instance Virgil's

et jam summa procul villarum culmina fumant
majoresque cadunt altis de montibus umbrae.

And now afar off the smoke ascends from the cottage-roofs, and from the high mountains the larger shadows fall.

But there is nothing in this description to *differentiate* this particular sunset from other sunsets. Shadows always creep down mountains at sunset and smoke always rises. It is the form rather than the content of these lines which appeals to us. I wonder, by the way, if there has ever been an ardent Virgilian who could not read Latin. I doubt it. Virgilian music evaporates in translation and only those who can read him in the original can fully appreciate the contrast between Virgil and the lesser Latin poets—Ennius, for instance, who could write,

Septingenti sunt paulo aut minus anni
Augusto augurio postquam incluta condita Roma est.

Whereas the Virgilian hexameters glide like a gondola along the lagoons of Venice these lines of Ennius are like a decrepit tram thudding and creaking over tramlines which need repairing.

Here is a Virgilian sunrise:

Jamque rubescebat radiis mare et aethere ab alto
Aurora in croceis fulgebat lutea bigis,
cum venti posuere omnisque repente resedit
flatus et in lento luctantur marmore tonsae.

And now the sea was blushing with the morning rays, and in the high heaven saffron Aurora shone in her golden car, when the winds dropped and every breath of air suddenly subsided, and the oars labour in the sluggish sea.

And here is Euripides' attempt to describe a sunrise:

Παρνησιάδες δ'ἄβατοι κορυφαί
καταλαμπόμεναι τὴν ἡμερίαν
ἁψῖδα βροτοῖσι δέχονται

The untrodden crests of Parnassus shine forth and welcome for mortals the orb of the new day.

Virgil's formal epithets and conventional mythology in the passage quoted might have occurred to a poet blind from birth, and there is nothing in the lines quoted from Euripides which could not be applied with equal felicity to any mountain dawn, whether seen from within the heart of a mountain range or from the distant plains.

Here is a passage from Belloc's *The Path to Rome*, which is not only one of the loveliest descriptions of a sunrise in all literature, but which has also the note of *differentiation*, in so far as he is concerned to evoke a picture not of sunrises in general but of a *southern* sunrise in particular:

> Then suddenly the sky grew lighter upon every side. That cheating gloom (which I think the clouds in purgatory must reflect) lifted from the valley as though to a slow order given by some calm and good influence that was marshalling in the day. Their colours came back to things; the trees recovered their shape, life, and trembling; here and there, on the face of the mountain opposite, the mists by their movement took part in the new life, and I thought I heard for the first time the tumbling water far below me in the ravine . . . There, without any warning of colours, or of the heraldry that we have in the north, the sky was a great field of pure light, and without doubt it was all woven through, as was my mind watching it, with security and gladness.

"It is a good thing", wrote Hilaire Belloc, "to have loved one woman from a child, and it is a good thing not to have to return to the Faith." What lured him back to the Church? Mainly perhaps his love for his wife, a devout American Catholic of Irish ancestry. Even in the days when he was little more than a nominal Catholic he never lost his profound reverence for the Church as the heir of the Graeco-Roman civilization. In North Africa he had chanced on an epitaph

> carved upon a tomb [writes Speaight] in memory of some priestess of Isis who had served the divinities of the woods so well that when she died "*ingemuerunt Dryades*". "Twice I read those delicate words, delicately chiselled in hard stone, and I saw her going in black, with her head bent, through groves." This was pagan antiquity and Belloc was perfectly at home in it.

The word pagan is derived from *paganus*, a countryman, for it was the conservative *pagani* with their *pietas* and their reverence for the traditional rites who were the last to accept the new religion, Christianity. It was this *pietas* which was the strength of paganism, the foundation of Rome in her greatest age. It is as grotesque for modern materialists who have no roots in the past, and no *pietas*, to describe themselves as pagans as it would be for a much married film star to borrow and appropriate for herself from classical antiquity the rank and style of a Vestal Virgin.

Belloc returned to the Faith because he was at home in pagan antiquity and therefore at home in that Catholic culture which has its roots not only in Bethlehem but also in the Graeco-Roman civilization which was the cradle of the Church. In *The Path to Rome* he describes his arrival in an Alsatian inn.

> . . . she also was Catholic—(she had a little tree set up before her door for the Corpus Christi: see what religion is, that makes people of utterly different races understand each other; for when I saw that tree I knew precisely where I stood. So once all we Europeans understood each other, but now we are divided by the worst malignancies of nations and classes, and a man does not so much love his own nation as hate his neighbours, and even the twilight of chivalry is mixed up with a detestable patronage of the poor. But as I was saying—) she also was a Catholic, and I knew myself to be with friends.

I was a young agnostic when I first read *The Path to Rome*, but this particular passage struck a responsive chord. The Catholic claims, I felt, were absurd and yet in this passage Belloc had expressed something which I too had felt. In the Catholic valleys of the Alps I felt at home. The Angelus bell, and the little mountain shrines, and the rude statue of some local saint in a mountain church, spoke to me in a language which was not mine, but which in some dim fashion I felt had once been mine. "I saw for a moment the Catholic Church quite plain, and I remembered Europe and the centuries." Long before I too saw the Church "quite plain", I had been reminded by Belloc of "Europe and the centuries". I was one of many who first discovered in Belloc's writings that sense of a European unity created by the Faith and destroyed by schism.

It was to the Church as the successor of the Roman Empire that Belloc owed allegiance. For Belloc the Church militant was no mere figure of speech. His loyalty to the Church had something in common with his loyalty to the regiment in which he had served as a conscript. He was once asked what would be his reaction if something which he had written were to be condemned by Rome. "I'd stand to attention," he replied, "and obey as a centurion would obey if some idiot of a commanding officer had issued a ridiculous command."

Belloc was a soldier of the Church militant and there were parts of our Lord's teaching which he probably found uncongenial, for the texts which pacifists love to quote did not appeal to the man who wrote,

Pale Ebenezer thought it wrong to fight
  But Roaring Bill (who killed him) thought it right.

Edward Shanks, the literary critic who described Belloc as "the greatest writer of English prose since Dryden", told me that Belloc once said to him, "I revere our Lord on the authority of the Church but as a Man he does not appeal to me." My knowledge of Belloc's writings seems to confirm the accuracy of Shanks' recollection, for I can only remember one passage in Belloc's writings—there may be many more—in which Belloc invokes our Lord, and this in the poem "In Praise of Wine",

> . . . so my Friend
> Let not Your cup desert me at the end . . .
> And sacramental, raise me the Divine:
> Strong brother in God and last companion, Wine.

Certainly Robert Speaight, who knew nothing of Belloc's remark to Shanks until some time after his book appeared, intuitively realized that Belloc avoided the words "Christian" and "Christianity". Indeed, Robert Speaight insists that "for Belloc 'Christianity' had practically no meaning; he was impatient with Christian sentiment unless it were controlled by dogma".

Belloc, who had a great devotion to the presence of our Lord in the Sacrament, would never have denied that this, the Church's central act of worship, is Christocentric, but the absence from his writings of any clear evidence of interest in or devotion to the human personality of Jesus of Nazareth helps to explain his failure to understand Protestantism, which is essentially Christocentric. His biographer, however, does well to remind us that "wherever he found a sincere Christian Faith he respected it, and he always held his old Wesleyan nurse, Sarah Mew, to be one of the saintliest people he had ever known".

Pius XI's reminder that Catholics are spiritually Semites can hardly have pleased Belloc. The Church, so Hilaire Belloc would have us believe, accepted the "traditional Hebrew books" because our Lord appealed to their authority, but "the decision of the Church to stand by the Jewish Scriptures was not maintained without difficulty. The documents were alien to that glorious civilization of the Mediterranean which the Church penetrated and transformed. Their diction was, in its ears, uncouth and irrational. The deeds they recounted (with approval) sounded barbaric and often absurd; taken as moral examples, some were found repulsive, others puerile; and the whole was of another and (to Greek and Roman) lesser and more degraded world".

It is odd that Belloc, who so constantly drew attention to the fact that the Church bases her claims on rational argument, did not realize that the Catholic is arguing most rationally when he begins by inviting the sceptic to approach the Old Testament with the judicial outlook of the scholar, to consider the evidence that God revealed himself to the Jews and gradually prepared them for the Incarnation, to examine every possible hypothesis for the Empty Tomb and to consider the alternative explanations to the Resurrection. It is only when he has accepted on the evidence, and on the evidence alone, the fact that Jesus of Nazareth proved his divine claims by rising from the dead and that he founded a Church to teach in his name, that he has rational grounds for accepting any dogmas on the authority of the Church. So far, then, from accepting our Lord and the Old Testament on the authority of the Church, we accept the Church as the deduction from our reading of the Old Testament and the New.

On the other hand the appeal to reason is implicit in Belloc's apologetic for the Church. I remember being infuriated by his confident assertion that only a Catholic can understand history, but I ended by realising that whether this be or be not an overstatement, the Catholic explanation of history makes sense as nothing else does. The rational arguments which led Belloc to the Catholic conclusion were reinforced by his intuition of holiness as something inexplicable if we deny the supernatural. For Belloc holiness was a sixth proof of the existence of God: "He did not in the least run after holy people but when he met them he felt the contact—as hard and as real as a rock. It was the conviction of sanctity which bound him to Father Vincent McNabb and he would go anywhere to hear him speak."

Belloc's devotion to our Lady was the inspiration of his noblest poetry. His unquestioning faith in the power of her intercession was expressed in the moving letter which he wrote to Chesterton on his conversion. Belloc went to Mass whenever he could but confessed that "the modern habit of very frequent Communion came too late to capture me". He never read spiritual books, and there is no record that he went to a retreat after leaving the Oratory. He had little or no understanding of mysticism.

> . . . I was never made for understanding this "union with God" business: St. Theresa and the rest. I don't know what it is all about and the description of isolation and detachment, "the necessary night of the soul", disgusts me like Wagner's music or boiled mutton. Good for others: not for me. I am no more fitted to it than is an elephant for caviare, or a dog for irony.[1]

There is however something akin to mystical experience in his famous description of the vision of the distant Alps from the Weissenstein.

> From the height of the Weissenstein I saw, as it were, my religion . . . the great peaks made communion between that homing creeping part of me which loves vineyards and dances and a slow movement among pastures and that other part which is only properly at home in heaven. . . . These, the great Alps seen thus, link one in some way to one's immortality.

[1] Letter to Mrs. Raymond Asquith, 23 Feb. 1927.

All that nature mysticism has in common with authentic mysticism is an intuition of supernatural beauty as reflected in the temporal loveliness of the world, but even so it is surprising that Belloc's quasi-mystical experience on the Weissenstein did not provide him with some clue to the experiences of the great mystics.

Belloc seldom enjoyed the happiness of *feeling* himself to be in touch with the divine.

> It is not as though I had any vision, comprehension or sense of the Divine Order . . . I am by all my nature of mind sceptical, by all my nature of body sensual. So sensual that the virtues restrictive of sense are but phrases to me. *But I accept these phrases as true and act upon them as well as a struggling man can.* . . . I like to hear from the lips of others, as though it were a thing seen, *that which I know I must defend but to which I have no access of my own* . . . in the matter of religion I am abominably alone. *I feel sometimes like a sentry at night.* [Italics mine.]

Protestants tend to blur the all-important distinction between religious *feeling* and religious *experience*. My Methodist uncle told me that as a young man he was often unhappy because however hard he tried he never really *felt* that he was saved. To the Catholic religious *feeling* is an extra, something we have no right to demand. Many saints were for long periods of their lives without any religious feeling and denied the consolation which others found in prayer and in praise. The Catholic knows that religious experience is the reward of the struggle against temptation and of the practice, however imperfect, of virtue. As Robert Speaight has well said,

> The Christian experience is precisely the exercise of the theological virtues—faith, hope and charity—

> and we estimate a man's Christianity by the degree to which he appears to practise them. Judged by these standards, no one who knew Belloc would say that he was without experience of the religion which he preached. . . . Like every other man, he had his faults. But it is not often that one can say of a man of genius, quite simply, that he was a good man. One can say of Belloc not only that he was good, but that he was supernaturally good. The "experience" that was not apparent to him was apparent to other people—and that is the test.

And however much and however often he might feel "alone and unfed", few Catholics have excelled him in the power to convey to others the fruits of religious experience. No man without that experience could have written one of the noblest passages ever written in defence of the Faith:

> For what is the Catholic Church? It is that which replies, co-ordinates, establishes. It is that within which is right order; outside, the puerilities and the despairs. It is a grasp upon reality. Here alone is promise, and here alone a foundation.
>
> Those of us who boast so stable an endowment make no claim thereby to personal grace; we are not saved thereby alone. But we are of so glorious a company that we receive support, and have communion. The Mother of God is also ours. Our dead are with us. Even in these our earthly miseries we always hear the distant something of an eternal music, and smell a native air. There is a standard set for us whereto our whole selves respond, which is that of an inherited and endless life, quite full, in our own country.[1]

[1] "A Letter to Dean Inge", reprinted in *Essays of a Catholic*, Sheed and Ward, 1931.

"He welcomed", writes Speaight, "the adhesion of Hollis and Arnold Lunn to the ranks of his fellow combatants. They did something to relieve his loneliness. But their fidelity did not guarantee the truth of every private attitude or interpretation. His disciples created an orthodoxy, which was their manner of being Catholics, as it was his, and there is no need to reproach them for it."

This passage suggests a more uncritical discipleship than the facts warranted. With much that he wrote I agreed, with much I disagreed. His interpretation of history was, as I gradually discovered, sounder than that of most contemporary historians, but there was truth in his candid reply to Father Philip Hughes' question why he refused to give references: "I am not a historian. I am a publicist." He was a splendid advocate but he was not judicial, and he often ignored facts which told against one of his pet theories. My confidence in his judgement was badly shaken by his persistence in maintaining that the battle between the political parties was nothing but a sham battle, and still more by his refusal, to the end of his days, to admit that Dreyfus was innocent. At one time I made a detailed study of the Dreyfus case, and though I share Belloc's dislike of the more unsavoury of Dreyfus's supporters, many of whom were later active in the campaign to drive the religious Orders out of France and the priests from the schools, I was disedified by Belloc's refusal to reconsider his belief in Dreyfus's guilt, which may have been tenable at the time of the first trial, but which ceased to be tenable in the light of later revelations.

If, however, on this occasion Belloc was obstinate in the defence of an unpopular falsehood—the falsehood that Dreyfus was guilty—let us remember to his lasting credit that he devoted most of his life to the active defence of unpopular truths. He would have had a far easier life, and have been less plagued by financial troubles, had he been content to insinuate an occasional hint of his Catholic beliefs instead of continuing to attack popular errors and continuing no less defiantly to proclaim his own militant Catholicism. When he rose to address the first meeting in the constituency which he later represented in Parliament he began,

> Gentlemen, I am a Catholic. As far as possible, I go to Mass every day. This [taking a rosary out of his pocket] is a rosary. As far as possible, I kneel down and tell these beads every day. If you reject me on account of my religion, I shall thank God that he has spared me the indignity of being your representative.

His integrity, for which he paid a heavy cost, was the more creditable because there was much truth in his jesting confession,

> I'm tired of Love: I'm still more tired of Rhyme
> But Money gives me pleasure all the time.

But this pleasure never took priority of the pleasure which he derived from proclaiming unpopular truths. Belloc would have had a far easier life had he been prepared to come to terms with a world which is ready enough to condone Catholicism in the unaggressive Catholic. He would have made more money had he toned down his advocacy of unfashionable truths.

> But there were many things he might have sold
> And would not sell.

The aggressive aspect of Belloc's apologetics was important. He undermined the Whig legend. He gave confidence to the Catholic minority in England, with the result that none of those who were familiar with his work could fail to realise that there was no substance in those attacks on the Faith which seemed so formidable to the "Pale Ebenezers" in the Catholic body.

Robert Speaight's biography crowns Belloc's achievement as an apologist, for private letters hitherto unpublished help us to understand and appreciate Belloc's own inner life as a Catholic. Some of these letters, in which Belloc writes sadly of his own lack of religious feeling, are invaluable reading for all those who write in defence of the Faith, and in particular for those who might otherwise be unduly discouraged by their own limitations, for those who, like Belloc, "know without feeling" that the Church is what the Church claims to be.

In his emphasis on reason and in his distrust of emotion, Belloc was the apologist for an age which has witnessed the revolt against reason. He helps us to realise that the Faith represents not the triumph of emotion over reason but the defeat of emotional scepticism by rational argument. Our emotions too often play the role of a Fifth Column in the citadel of belief, conspiring with the besieging army to surrender the fortress of faith.

Consider, for instance, the cardinal doctrine of immortality. It is to the emotions rather than to the mind that the unbroken silence of the dead makes so strong an appeal. The conviction that they survive is the conclusion of a chain of rational argument which one may *feel* to be false but which one *knows* to be true.

I remember so well the first time that I looked upon the face of a friend who was dead, a friend who had fallen to his death on a Pyrenean peak. At the time I neither believed nor disbelieved in immortality but I remember *feeling* that this was final, for nothing could look more invincibly mortal than what was left of that gallant mountaineer, and no *emotional* appeal to scepticism could have been stronger than the appeal of that broken and disfigured body. If I had continued to trust solely to my emotions and to my feeling I should, perhaps, still disbelieve in immortality, but I can now say with Belloc,

> . . . as to the doubt of the soul I discover it to be false: a mood: not a conclusion. My conclusion—and that of all men who have ever once *seen* it—is the Faith: Corporate, organised, a personality, teaching. A thing, not a theory. It.
>
> To you, who have the blessing of profound religious emotion, this statement may seem too desiccate. It is indeed not enthusiastic. It lacks meat.
>
> It is my misfortune. In youth I had it: even till lately. Grief has drawn the juices from it. I am alone and unfed, the more do I affirm the Sanctity, the Unity, the Infallibility of the Catholic Church. By my very isolation do I the more affirm it, as a man in a desert knows that water is right for man: or as a wounded dog, not able to walk yet knows the way home. . . .
>
> But beyond this there will come in time, if I save my soul, the flesh of these bones—which bones alone I can describe and teach. I know—without feeling (an odd thing in such a connection) the reality of Beatitude: which is the goal of Catholic Living.
>
> In hac urbe lux sollennis
> Ver eternum pax perennis
> Et eterna gaudia.[1]

[1] Letter to Chesterton, August 1922.

VI

"SURVIVALS AND NEW ARRIVALS"

I HAVE borrowed my title from a book in which Hilaire Belloc analyses the "survivals", that is, the attacks on the Church which had lost their old effectiveness and were in the process of being quietly dropped, and the "new arrivals", that is, the more modern lines of attack.

In Chapter VII I shall discuss a Victorian survival, the attack which takes for its starting point an alleged conflict between science and religion, an attack which has lost much of its old vigour. Chapter VIII is devoted to some afterthoughts on the Spanish Civil War, which provided our enemies with a pretext for accusing us of clerico-fascism. Fascism and Nazism have been destroyed in the countries of their origin, and atheistic Communism is not only the implacable foe of the Catholic Church but also of all those values in which the democracies of the West profess to believe. Rome, England, and America have the same mortal enemy and some of those who remember how consistently the Church has opposed Communism, and who realize that alone of the Christian communions it has been wholly unaffected by Communist infiltration, are beginning to wonder whether the Pope, though clearly not infallible, is not perhaps remarkably well informed. At a time when both the Americans and the British were flirting with Italian Communism, the influence of the Catholic Church was decisive in the elections which saved Italian democracy from a victory for the Communist front, and this has made it increasingly difficult to maintain the idiotic pretence that there is a necessary antagonism between the Church and democracy.

So much for the principal "survivals". The "new arrival" is not wholly new and is indeed merely a reinforced variant of an old "survival", the neo-Malthusian campaign for the limitation of families. All that is new is the change from a slightly defensive attitude to militant attacks on those who still persist in having big families.

A hundred years ago large families were still the norm, small the exception. My father, for instance, was the eldest of a family of twelve. In the next phase the Protestant upper and middle class began to limit their families but they none the less had a genuine admiration for those who did not. That phase has passed. Today the small family is regarded as natural, the large family as unnatural, and before long the parent of large families will be criticized as anti-social. The natural resources of the world, we are assured, are being rapidly exhausted and we have begun to tread "The Road to Scarcity", to quote the title of a famous book. The large family is therefore consuming more than its fair share of the available food resources. It is easy to foresee the enthusiasm with which the anti-Catholics will exploit this line of attack on the Church.

And yet it is only a few years since the pundits insisted that the real problem of the world was not scarcity but abundance. Indignant Socialists denounced the destruction of food in the New World, wheat and coffee, for instance, to keep up prices, while in other parts of the globe men were starving. Capitalism had clearly been proved to be inefficient by its incapacity to distribute the good things which bounteous nature provided. "Starving in the midst of plenty" was the slogan of all progressive anti-capitalists. "Gorging in the midst of starvation" may yet prove to be the slogan of progressive anti-Catholics.

Modern life is more and more adjusted to the requirements of the small family. A friend of mine who was about to be married was going to see a flat with his fiancée. The agent took him aside and murmured in a tactful whisper, "Excuse me mentioning it, Sir, but babies aren't born in these flats. It's against the rules." Limitation of families is not confined to Protestants; Catholics, it is said, average only one child more per family than Protestants in England and America. A small family is, however, often the result of voluntary restraint and sometimes of the apparent tendency for families which have lived for more than three generations in a town to become sterile.

When I was working in Germany for the American State Department just after the War there was an acute housing shortage and many young married couples were, as in England, living with their in-laws in overcrowded conditions. I asked a priest what he felt about young couples who confessed to contraception and who might only too easily lapse again.

"Our task", he said, "is not to lose contact with them. If we keep them in the Church, their children will be brought up as Catholics. There are conditions which call for heroic virtue in a young married couple, if the Church's laws on marriage are to be observed. Heroic virtue is rare, not perhaps so rare as you might think, but we have to keep the way of return open even for those who lack heroic virtue."

Many Catholics leave the Church because they find the Catholic code too exacting, and most of those who leave lose all contact with religion, for it is only a small minority who become practising members of other Christian communions. Some become "back-pew Catholics", that is, Catholics who are regular in their assistance at Mass but who do not communicate. The typical back-pew Catholic is the Catholic who has made an irregular marriage. There are no back-pew Protestants, for the Protestant Churches do not refuse the sacraments to remarried divorcees. The back-pew Catholic might almost be described as a negative note of the Church, for his continual loyalty to a Church which denies him the sacraments is an impressive tribute to the objective truths which the Church proclaims. There is, of course, no reason why the brain should soften because the flesh is weak. The back-pew Catholic by his presence at Mass affirms his conviction that the Catholic code has not ceased to be valid merely because he has found it too exacting. By his loyalty to the Church which denies him the sacraments he is affirming his respect for the virtue of intellectual integrity.

Those apostles of the new morality, for instance, who try to give the impression that they have examined the case against the traditional code of sexual morals with detachment, and that they have reached their amoral conclusions with the scientific objectivity of an unbiased historian, lack the basic virtue of intellectual integrity. They are preaching what they practise, the ultimate hypocrisy. The Victorians, so often and so falsely accused of hypocrisy, seldom practised what they preached, for inevitably the behaviour of the average Christian falls far short of the ideal, but if the ideal itself is discredited the main barrier to moral nihilism is removed, and it is for this reason that the Church has always been more disturbed by deviations from orthodox doctrine than by deviations from orthodox morals. As long as the doctrine is not questioned moral lapses are recognized for what they are.

"If a priest goes morally wrong," a Jesuit once remarked to me, "the authorities are of course distressed and every effort is made to save him from the shipwreck of his faith. There is a routine for dealing with this sort of problem. If, however, a flavour of heresy is detected in anything a priest writes or says, there's a terrific flap not only among his own superiors but in Rome. However innocuous heresy may seem in its embryo stage, its possibilities for doing harm are unlimited."

As he spoke I remembered Luther's bitter comment on those who had followed him out of the Church into schism: "Who would have begun to preach," he exclaimed in 1539, "had we known before that so much misfortune, scandal, slander, thanklessness and wickedness would follow? But as we are in it we must hold on."[1]

Any discussion with non-Catholics of the Church's attitude to contraception is complicated by the fact that the very idea of sin as an offence against God is vanishing from our civilization, and is being replaced by a pragmatic criterion which judges sin solely by its obvious effects on other people, condemning sins which can be *proved* to have mischievous social consequences and condoning those which *appear* to have no such consequences. I can illustrate the difficulty of getting our point of view across by a disconcerting experience when lecturing in Australia. A non-Catholic in the audience asked me to defend the Church's attitude to birth control. After vainly trying to explain that it was wrong to take steps to defeat the main (but not the only) purpose for which the sexual act had been ordained, I continued:

"The consequences of sin can be traced even in the natural order. There is an inevitable tendency for races

[1] See *The Revolt Against Reason*, p. 62.

with large families to replace races which practise family limitation. The Greek historian Polybius insisted that the main reason for the defeat of Greece by Rome was that the Greeks limited their families by infanticide.

"Nineteen centuries later Pétain echoed Polybius and explained France's defeat by the fact that too few babies had been born. Cartagena in the Caribbean was once a predominantly white city, a Spanish colony with a minority of negro slaves. Today the whites are in a very small minority. We can follow the same evolution in New York. Harlem was once inhabited by whites. Today not only the negroes but the Puerto Ricans are pushing their frontiers down-town. I remember a priest remarking wistfully, 'I wonder whether one day people will say "It's odd to think that New York was once a white city".' Fifty years ago a Bostonian of the old Yankee stock preaching to his Protestant congregation said, 'If you of the old American stock continue to have small families Boston will one day be ruled by the descendants of your Irish servants and workers.' And this prediction has come true.

"There is a curious parallel between pacificism and contraception. If every nation simultaneously disarmed none would be overrun, but in practice the first to disarm often becomes the victim of those who have not disarmed. Similarly with contraception. If the limitation of families was as common in Asia as it is in Australia the threat to your white Australia would be less serious."

Next morning I opened the local paper to discover that "Mr. Lunn said that contraception would be all right if only we could convert the Asiatics to contraception". The reporter, poor chap, had done his best and no man can do more, but it would be just as reasonable to expect an

Australian cricket reporter to produce a technically correct report of the first game of Pelota that he had ever seen as to hope that the average product of a secular education would understand an attempt to relate theology to its consequences in the natural order.

VII

THE CONFLICT BETWEEN SCIENCE AND SCIENTISM

WE ARE indebted to some anonymous benefactor for the useful word "scientism" to describe the views of those who maintain that science has disproved the existence of the supernatural and the possibility of miracles. In effect the scientians (that is, those who accept scientism) believe that the physical universe is coterminous with reality.

Scientism was perhaps the most important of the many influences which transformed England from a country which still had some claim to be Christian into modern England, in which any such claim would be patently ridiculous. The scientians would have been far less successful had the Christians, both Catholic and Protestant, been less ineffective in putting their case before the public.

The first blunder of the Christians was terminological. They allowed the scientians to pose as the champions of science, a pose which would have been far less easy to make convincing if the word "scientism" had been invented when the controversy began. Unfortunately the damage had been done before this useful word, which even today is not in general use, made its first appearance in print. Archbishop Trench writes:

> The success and enduring influence of any systematic construction of truth depends as much on an exact

terminology as upon close and deep thinking itself. "Terms", says Whewall, "record discoveries . . ." Hardly any original thoughts assume their proper importance even in the minds of the inventors until aptly selected words and phrases have nailed them down and held them fast.

Because the Christians failed to differentiate between scientists and scientians they made it easy for the scientians to pose as the champions of science and to popularize the conception of conflict between science and religion. There is no such conflict, but there is a very real conflict between religion and scientism and between science and atheism.

We believe in miracles because and *only because* we believe in science. It is because we have faith in the scientific knowledge of the medical scientists who investigate the alleged miracles at Lourdes that we can assert with confidence that certain cures, which no doctor can explain, may be miraculous.

The second blunder of the Christians was their failure adequately to challenge the basic assumption of scientism, the assumption that scientians appeal to science and to reason. Whereas St. Thomas Aquinas starts from one modest assumption that "it is certain and obvious to the senses that some things are in motion", and *proves* by rational argument that God exists, the scientian *assumes* that ultimate reality is coterminous with the physical universe, *assumes* that the supernatural is a figment of man's mind, and *assumes* that miracles are impossible.

St. Thomas Aquinas was a rationalist in the correct sense of that much abused word. The scientian is a fideist. The Church condemned as fideists those who denied the power of unaided human reason to reach certitude, and who affirmed that the fundamental act of human knowledge consisted of an act of faith. The scientians are fideists for, unlike the Catholics, they offer no reasoned argument in defence of their basic beliefs. "To this day," wrote that distinguished mathematical philosopher the late Professor A. N. Whitehead, F.R.S., "science has remained an anti-intellectualist movement based on a naïve faith." A statement which is certainly true of the scientians, who exploited the prestige of science in support of their naïve faith.

The third blunder of the Christians was the failure to rub in the fact that the basic assumptions of the scientian were not only unproved but unprovable. That distinguished Frenchman, Professor Richet, was a sceptic but he was not a fideist, he was prepared to investigate unfashionable phenomena such as those alleged to be produced by mediums. "Why should there not be intelligent and puissant beings", he asked, "distinct from those perceptible to the senses? By what right should we dare to affirm on the basis of our limited senses, our defective intellect, and our scientific past, as yet hardly three centuries old, that in the vast cosmos man is the sole intelligent being, and that all mental reality always depends upon new cells irrigated by oxygenated blood?"

Neither the philosopher nor the scientist can advance a single argument against the possibility that God exists and that God, if he exist, can suspend those alleged laws of nature which owe their existence to him. The question, therefore, whether miracles occur is a question to be decided by, and only by, the evidence. The scientian axiom that science forbids us to believe in miracles betrays a fundamental misunderstanding of the scope of science. As indeed T. H. Huxley himself realized, for Huxley admitted that the great progress of science in the nineteenth century had in no way weakened the case for theism.

> The philosophical difficulties of theism [he wrote] are neither greater nor less than they have been ever since theism was invented. . .

Huxley conceded that "'creation' in the ordinary sense of the term is perfectly conceivable", and that "the *a priori* arguments against theism, and, given a deity, against the possibility of creative acts, appear to me devoid of reasonable foundation."

The fourth blunder of the Christians was the failure to drive home the fact that scientists in general seemed to have no criterion for assessing the relative importance of different fields of research. It is only a small minority of scientists who have given priority to those forms of research which are concerned with a problem infinitely more important than most of those which scientists attempt to solve, the problem as to whether matter was created by a spiritual Creator or whether all mental and spiritual processes are the by-product of matter. Upon our answer to this question depends the validity of scientific research. If materialism be true, then all our beliefs, including our scientific beliefs, are due to the blind operation of materialistic causes. "On that hypothesis," as Arthur Balfour rightly said, "we no more possess free reason than we possess free will. As all our volitions are the inevitable product of forces which are quite alien to morality, so all our conclusions are the inevitable product of forces which are quite alien to reason."

"Theism", as Balfour pointed out in *The Foundations of Belief*, "is a principle which science therefore requires for its own completion", and even if this were not the case it would not be unreasonable to expect scientists to accord high priority to any form of research which might provide a clue to the riddle of the grave. But whereas any scientist who helps to reduce the death rate and to prolong life would receive generous recognition, scientists who investigate evidence for the claim that life is prolonged beyond the grave lose caste with their fellow scientists and damage their careers. Sir Oliver Lodge, for instance, in all probability would have been elected President of the Royal Society but for his interest in spiritualism. Dr. Alexis Carrel, a distinguished scientist and Nobel Prize winner, fully realized the risks which he took when, as a young doctor, he decided to investigate the miracles at Lourdes. He was an agnostic when he visited Lourdes but an agnostic who realized, in his own words, that "science has to explore the entire realm of reality", including those realms which the intellectual fashion of the day regarded as definitely non-U. He tells us that he began his study of the Lourdes miracles "at a time when it was difficult for a young doctor and *dangerous for his future career* to be interested in such a subject". The words which I have italicized are evidence that scientists suspected of scientific heresy must expect persecution, and that the kind of snobbery which consists in timid conformity to the intellectual fashion of the moment is as widespread in the world of science as in the world of society. Dr. Carrel ruined his career in France by his scientific interest in Lourdes, and was grateful to the Rockefeller Institute of New York, which offered him a position. He demonstrated his intellectual courage and intellectual integrity by publishing his conclusion that miraculous cures were facts of which science had to take account. Here is the relevant passage from his famous book *Man the Unknown* (p. 155):

> Miraculous cures seldom occur. Despite their small number they prove the existence of organic and mental processes that we do not know. They show that certain mystic states, such as that of prayer, have definite effects. *They are stubborn irreducible facts, which must be*

taken into account. The author knows that miracles are as far from scientific orthodoxy as mysticity. The investigation of such phenomena is still more delicate than that of telepathy and clairvoyance. *But science has to explore the entire realm of reality.* [Italics mine.]

Lourdes is not only the greatest challenge to materialism and to its camouflage, scientism, but it is also a criterion to distinguish between the sceptic whose approach to this problem is scientific and the sceptic who refuses to examine any evidence which conflicts with the simple dogmas of his scientian faith. The former may be recommended to read Jean Hellé's book on miracles from which I have already quoted, *Miracles Still Happen* by B. G. Sandhurst, *The Medical Proof of the Miraculous* by Le Bec, *The Meaning of Lourdes* by Izard or *Raisons Médicales de Croire au Miracle* by Leuret. And if the sceptic regards all these books as suspect because they are written by Catholics, may I commend to him *Science and the Supernatural*, my published controversy with Professor J. B. S. Haldane, F.R.S., in which Haldane argues the case against the supernatural in general and miracles in particular.

Among the many cases which I cited in our controversy the most striking was perhaps the case of Peter de Rudder, a Belgian farm labourer whose leg was shattered by the fall of a tree. Seven years passed and the bones did not unite. De Rudder continued obstinately to resist the advice of his doctors, who recommended amputation. He determined to ask his cure from our Lady of Lourdes, venerated at the shrine of Oostaker near Antwerp. The broken leg was instantaneously cured. The condition of his leg before entering the shrine was described by his doctor, a sceptic converted to Christianity by this miracle, in an affidavit: "I have examined De Rudder a dozen times and my last visit was two or three months before the cure. Each time I was able to make the ends of the bones come out of the wound. They were deprived of their periosteum, there was necrosis, the suppuration was fetid and abundant . . ." The medical evidence was confirmed by the witnesses who saw De Rudder a few days before the cure and by the driver of the tram on which he travelled from Antwerp to Oostaker and who made a joke at his expense. "There goes a man who is going to lose his leg."

Haldane did not accept the miraculous hypothesis but made one notable concession: "I think that the odds were that the bones were united, and the septic wounds healed, in a few hours, the most probable alternative being a pious fraud enacted by a large number of people. The only remarkable element in the cure is its speed." But it is precisely the *speed* of the cure which is evidence of the miraculous nature of the cure.

A brief note on the investigation of these cures is desirable. A patient who claims to have been miraculously cured, hereinafter termed "the claimant", is examined first by the Bureau of Scientific Studies. The co-operation of any doctor, irrespective of his religion, is welcomed by this bureau. Protestants, Mohammedans and atheists have served on the examining committees. If there be an *a priori* case for the claim, the claimant is urged to return next year, as the bureau never pronounces judgement until a year has elapsed.

Meanwhile the claimant is put in the care of the International Association of our Lady of Lourdes, which was founded in 1927 and which now numbers over four thousand members from every country in Europe and many from other continents. The association arranges for a member or members to watch the claimant during the year's wait before he returns to Lourdes for re-examination, and to keep his dossier up to date with evidence provided by his medical advisers. Next year a member of this association returns with the patient and brings with him a summary of the professional opinion and, if necessary, X-ray plates. The final court of appeal, a Second Chamber, is the International Committee, which consists of distinguished doctors, all Catholics. The International Committee initiates nothing, and never deals with an allegedly miraculous cure until it has been passed by the bureau as incapable of a natural explanation. The word "miracle" is never used from the moment the claim is made until the claim is accepted, and acceptance of the claim means no more than that the final court of appeal endorses the findings of the bureau to the effect that there is no natural explanation of the cure. When this international committee comes to the conclusion that the cure is beyond scientific explanation the papers are sent to the Bishop of Lourdes, who may forward them to the claimant's own bishop, and he in turn will then summon a canonical commission to re-examine the case once again. Acting upon their report the bishop may, if he thinks fit, pronounce the cure miraculous. Even then the individual Catholic is free to accept or to reject the miraculous hypothesis.

Even the sceptic must agree that the procedure adopted to test such claims is conscientious and thorough. Since 1920, when this detailed process of investigation was adopted, over two hundred and fifty claims for miraculous cures have been accepted.

The accumulated evidence for the supernatural at Lourdes, and for the preternatural phenomena of spiritualism, has had a steadily erosive effect on scientism.

Thirty years ago I made a thorough study of the literature of psychical research and thanks to my friendship with Sir Arthur Conan Doyle and Sir Oliver Lodge, F.R.S., I enjoyed unusual opportunities for attending séances with famous mediums. I witnessed various psychical phenomena, ectoplasm, movement of objects at a distance, etc. As a result of these experiences and above all of the record of séances carried out under the most exacting conditions by distinguished scientists I came to the following conclusions.

1. 95% of the allegedly preternatural phenomena are explicable as the result of hallucination, fraud, or malobservation.
2. The evidence for a residue of genuine preternatural phenomena, extra-sensory perception, materialization (ectoplasm), telekinesis (movement of objects at a distance), is far stronger than that for many beliefs which scientists accept without question.
3. Preternatural phenomena *may* be caused by spiritual beings.
4. Communication with the dead has *not* been proved.

When I began these investigations I should have welcomed evidence in support of the spiritualistic thesis that we can communicate with the dead. My negative conclusions were published many years before I became a Catholic, and could not therefore be explained, as spiritualist periodicals frequently do explain them, as imposed upon me by the authority of the Church.

I should have found it easier to accept the spiritualist hypothesis but for the depressing fact that the intellectual level of the spirits seemed so much lower than the intelligence of spirits incarnate in human flesh. It would seem, if spiritualism be true, that the dead suffer a rapid mental deterioration. It is, however, only fair to record the effective rejoinder of the Duchess of Hamilton on this particular point. Joad and I had been invited to explain to an audience of spiritualists why we were unconvinced by the evidence for spirit communication. I commented on the banality of the utterances alleged to emanate from the departed spirits, but the Duchess of Hamilton, who was in the chair, came back with a devastating rejoinder. "Naturally we get into touch with spirits of our own spiritual and cultural level." Clearly I am the sort of person who does not mix with the best spirits either in this world or in the next.

It is, however, only fair to record one communication from the spirit world which seemed to me wholly convincing. The story was told to me by a great friend of mine, Adrian, a convinced spiritualist.

"My friend Bob", said Adrian, "was assured by his spirit guide that he would never be killed by a bomb, and he used to wander about the streets during the big raids without a tremor."

In May 1941 Adrian was invited by Bob to attend a most important meeting in an upper room. It was, so Bob assured him, going to be like the Day of Pentecost and there would be a tremendous spiritual impact from the next world. Luckily for Adrian he was ill—luckily, for the impact was tremendous all right, but it was not a spiritual impact. Bob, whose spirit guide had assured him that he was immune to bombs, and all the faithful assembled in that upper room, were wiped out in an exceptionally heavy raid.

"I'd be intrigued", I remarked, "to have a first-hand account of what Bob said to his spirit guide when they met in the beyond. Did you ever get in touch with him?"

"Well . . . yes."

"What did Bob say?" I asked.

"Oh, nothing of any importance", said Adrian. His

reluctance to pursue the subject encouraged me to persist. What was he hiding?

"Come, now, Adrian, surely he was entitled to a handsome apology from his spirit guide. Did you raise the point with him?"

"Actually I did say that he seemed to have been let down."

"And what did Bob reply?"

"Nothing much. All he said was, 'So that's that.'"

My own study of spiritualist literature convinced me that wishful thinking determines the nature of most spirit communication. The spirits reveal what the spiritualists wish to hear. Thus up to the very outbreak of the Second World War the spirit guides were all agreed that there would be no war. Now of course there is no reason why spirits should be infallible in their predictions of the future, but it is surely disconcerting to find that their ability to foresee the shape of things to come is so far inferior to that of the living. Whereas most of those who had any knowledge of world affairs regarded war as probable after Hitler had occupied Prague, no spirit guide would admit the possibility of hostilities. Not one spirit guide predicted (as did the present writer in an article published in May 1939) the possibility of a Nazi-Russian pact, and whereas my lucky shot attracted no attention, had a spirit guide brought off that particular prediction it would have become a *locus classicus* in spiritualist literature. Those who consulted mediums wanted to be told that there would be no war and the spirits did not disappoint them.

An even more striking example of the influence of wishful thinking on spirit revelations was provided by the attempts to get in touch with Mallory and Irvine after they disappeared on Everest in the 1924 attempt. Everybody who had followed the Everest attempts would have been delighted to discover that they had reached the summit. "The mystery of this accident", I wrote to Sir Oliver Lodge, "provides spiritualists with a unique opportunity of demonstrating communication with the dead. Though it has been demonstrated that mediums in trance often reveal knowledge of facts which they had no normal means of knowing, this could be explained by telepathy between the medium and the sitters, but as no human being knows what happened to Mallory and Irvine, telepathy between the living and the dead would be no explanation of information about their last moments. If the accuracy of this information were confirmed by a subsequent expedition the evidence for spirit communication would be irresistible. We are assured again and again by the spirits that the departed are only too anxious to provide us with convincing proofs of their survival and thus to liberate men from the fear of death. Here then is an ideal opportunity to provide a decisive proof of survival."

Sir Oliver Lodge was impressed by the importance of this test case and for some months after I wrote he continued to send me the record of sittings at which Mallory and Irvine had described their last hours on Everest. On one point all these spirit messages were in agreement. Mallory and Irvine were killed on the descent after reaching the summit of Everest. We now know that they were killed on the ascent. An ice axe has been found which marks the place where the accident occurred. One climber must have slipped, and the other climber must have immediately dropped the axe to seize the rope in an attempt to check the fall. That they died on the ascent is clear, for once they reached the point from which they fell they could not have failed to have noted the far easier and shorter line which they would certainly have followed on the descent.

Now let us suppose that the spirits of the dead, who by hypothesis are so anxious to convince the world that men survive the grave, had communicated through mediums information as to where this axe would be found, it would be difficult for even the most sceptical to deny that accurate information about the last hours of these Everest adventurers had reached this world from the next.

One can reject, as I reject, the doctrines of spiritualism and yet recognize without qualification the great debt which the world owes to the pioneers of psychical research. Men like Oliver Lodge were undeterred by that subtler form of persecution with which orthodox scientists discourage the modern Galileos from experimenting with the non-U varieties of scientific research. The pioneers, by their devotion to what they believed to be true, have made it possible for modern investigators such as Professor Rhine of Duke University to conduct his experiments in extrasensory perception not only without opposition from his university but with the aid of a university grant.

I do not envy an old-fashioned materialist who attempts to reconcile the overwhelming evidence for telepathy and clairvoyance with the naïve dogmas of scientism. The waning influence of scientism is partially accounted for by the establishment of a scientific method of examining allegedly miraculous cures at Lourdes. In 1885 only five doctors were sufficiently courageous to defy the climate of scientific opinion by undertaking a journey of investigation to Lourdes. Today the number of doctors who visit Lourdes is seldom less than fifteen hundred a year. The increasing interest of the medical profession is reflected in the increase of space which popular papers devote to Lourdes. Some excellent articles on Lourdes appeared, for instance, in the *Daily Mail* during 1957.

It is unfortunately still only a minority who can be bothered to examine the evidence for the Lourdes miracles, but the fact that scientists have at last conceded that psychical research is at least a near-U form of scientific investigation has had a devastating effect on old-fashioned materialism. Finance is becoming an increasingly troublesome problem for *The Freethinker*, and the old-fashioned type of Victorian rationalist is gradually becoming extinct. Scientism is in fact a "survival" from the nineteenth century, and will in due course be relegated to a shelf in the storehouse of discarded philosophies.

NOTE

A very useful and well-documented book on the relation between religion and science is *The Church and Modern Science* by Patrick J. McLaughlin, B.D., D.Sc., Clonmore and Reynolds Ltd., Dublin, and Burns, Oates and Washbourne Ltd., London. The documentation is most useful as all the important Papal pronouncements on science, medical ethics, etc., are included.

The philosophy of scientism is discussed at great length in my book *The Revolt Against Reason*. The best possible defence of scientism will be found in Professor J. B. S. Haldane's letters in our joint book *Science and the Supernatural*. Both these books were published by Eyre & Spottiswoode in Great Britain and by Sheed & Ward in the U.S.A.

VIII

THE UNPOPULAR FRONT

If we adopt Hilaire Belloc's classification of attacks on the Church as "new arrivals" or "survivals", by far the most important "new arrival" since I became a Catholic was the popular charge that the Church was in essence clerico-fascist, the enemy of democracy and the covert ally of Fascism. It was the Spanish Civil War which appeared to give colour to this accusation in England and one result of that war was a sharp drop in conversions.

It is, of course, undeniable that most Catholics sympathized with those who rose in armed revolt to save their country from Communism. In 1944 I lectured to an American Bomber Group in Norfolk. At the end of my lecture a Jew asked me whether it was or was not true that the Pope had sympathized with what he called "the Spanish Fascists".

"When Hitler", I replied, "began to murder Jews, were your sympathies with Nazis or anti-Nazis?"

He made it clear that he thought this rather a silly question. "The answer to your question is obvious; with the anti-Nazis."

"Very well then, thousands of priests and nuns were murdered in Spain by your friends the Reds. Would you expect the sympathies of the Pope to be with the priests or with the murderers of the priests? Whatever your views may be, some of us are reactionary enough to believe that both Jews and priests should be given a sporting chance to die peacefully in their beds."

To the younger generation, of course, the Civil War is remote, and many of their seniors may be tempted to ask why I should be at pains to recall that bitter controversy. To which I reply that it is impossible to discuss the changing status of the Catholic Church during the quarter of a century which has passed since I became a Catholic without devoting some space to Spain, but I will do my best not to repeat the episodes described in earlier books, though I must of course reiterate certain conclusions.

It has been the destiny of Spain to give to the Church some of the Church's greatest saints and also to furnish the enemies of the Church with much of their ammunition. Torquemada is the main attraction in the Rogues' Gallery of Popery which is the delight of all good Protestants of the old school. The present régime in Spain, with its affinities to Fascism, is a boon to people like Paul Blanshard who are so anxious to prove that Catholicism is necessarily anti-democratic, and the foolish treatment of the Protestant minority in Spain is exploited to prove that the Church would revive the persecution of Protestants if ever she regained her ancient power.

Those Catholics—admittedly exceptional—who encourage their non-Catholic friends to state their objections to the Church, cannot afford to be ill-informed about Spain because sooner or later Spain will be introduced into the debate. That must be my excuse for this chapter.

My father was a Gladstonian Liberal. He believed in the inevitability of progress, in the gradual disappearance from the world of oppression and tyranny and in the predestined triumph of parliamentary government and all that was best in Liberalism. His confidence that sanity must triumph was only slightly shaken by those twin evils, Nazism and Communism. It was in this climate of optimism that my own philosophy of history was unconsciously formed. I remember as a young man reading the novels of Robert Hugh Benson in which he describes the execution and torture of the priests in Elizabethan England. That particular phase of human history, I felt, belonged to an evil past. Torquemada and the Elizabethan torturer Topcliffe were as extinct as the dodo.

As a Catholic, of course, I came under the influence of the realistic philosophy of the Church and yielded at least academic assent to the doctrine that there was no such thing as inevitable progress, but I did not finally discard the Utopian illusions of my youth until I climbed an observation tower on the Casa del Campo within view of besieged Madrid. As we reached the top of the tower the sun broke through the mist, gleamed on the long façade of the Palace and unshadowed the wounded frontage of the shell-shattered University City. And suddenly I realised that the dramas of Elizabethan England were being re-enacted in Madrid, that priests in hiding were celebrating Mass knowing well that if they were discovered or betrayed their names would be added to those of thousands of priests and nuns who had already died as martyrs in Red Spain. The Catholic cause in Spain was inevitably opposed by the kind of Protestant who finds atheists more congenial than Papists, and our difficulties were aggravated by the fact that Franco was supported by Hitler and Mussolini. All the financial resources of Spain—the gold, for instance, in the Bank of Spain—were at the disposal of the Republicans. The Nationalists would have been beaten in a few weeks had not a public-spirited American provided their army and air force with petrol and oil on credit. The present Government of Spain have not exactly gone out of their way to advertise their debt to this gentleman, who might almost be described as the Unknown Financier of the war. His name is Brewster. He comes from Texas, he is connected with the Texaco Company, and he is incidentally a Protestant, a fact which I commend to the notice of the Spanish Hierarchy.

The pressure on our Conservative Government to intervene against the Nationalists was never relaxed and some of the Conservative M.P.s with marginal seats were reluctant to incur the reproach of being branded as friends of Fascism. Spain owes a great debt to Mr. Neville Chamberlain for his firmness. It was at Mr. Chamberlain's suggestion, conveyed to me through Sir Arthur Bryant, that I went out to Spain to get material for my book *Spanish Rehearsal*, which was circulated to every Conservative M.P. and to Conservative Political Agents. The book had, I believe, a steadying effect.

All those who sympathized with the Republicans confidently predicted that Franco would fight against us if Hitler provoked a world war. Communists and fellow-travellers were bitterly disappointed by Franco's continued neutrality. Franco was greatly influenced in his decision to keep out of the War by the Infante Alfonso d'Orleans Bourbon, who was second-in-command of the Nationalist Air Force during the Civil War. The Infante had been educated in England—at Beaumont—and he married a British princess, daughter of Queen Victoria's second son, Alfred, Duke of Edinburgh, but the advice which he tendered to Franco was inspired far less by his genuine friendship for England than by his concern for the interests of his own country. I spent a fascinating week with him in September 1941 at Sanlucar and I remember how greatly I was heartened by his conviction that Hitler had lost the War.

"The result of this war", he said, "depended on the

Battle of Britain. Sooner or later America will enter the war. Hitler will be beaten."

I am inclined to believe that any inclination Franco might have had to intervene on the side of the Axis was more than neutralized by the German plot to eliminate him during the Civil War. It is curious how very little was known of this plot at the time, and how even now the inside story has never got into print. The fact that there was some such conspiracy was of course known and is mentioned by Mr. Peter Kemp in his excellent book, *Mine Were of Trouble*. He writes:

> . . . the Germans were anxious, for their own reasons, to see the war ended quickly. For some months they had been dissatisfied with General Franco, whose strategy they regarded as archaic and likely to lead to an indefinite prolongation of hostilities. But General Franco is a Gallago [Galician], with all the obstinacy and subtlety of that race; it was his war, and he was going to run it as he thought fit. The Germans therefore decided to replace him with a creature of their own; Señor Hedilla, as the leader of the most pro-German party, was their ideal tool. He was persuaded by General Faupel to stage a *coup d'état*, which very nearly succeeded. But General Franco reacted vigorously, suppressed the conspiracy, sent Hedilla to prison for ten years and demanded the recall of Faupel.

As Mr. Kemp justly remarks, the full details of this coup are "imperfectly known abroad". I can supplement Mr. Kemp's account with a few illuminating details. Shortly after the coup had taken place Serrano Suñer, who had been captured by the Reds, was exchanged for a prominent Red. Until he returned to Spain, General Franco had tended to favour the Requetés, the party of the Carlists. Suñer is said to have pointed out to him that Primo de Rivera was sent packing by the King and that Franco might expect the same fate if the monarchy were restored. Suñer advised him to make the Falange, a Spanish variant of Italian Fascism, the dominant party and himself the Spanish equivalent of the Duce.

Franco adopted this advice and at a later date restored to honour a Falangist (not Hedilla) who had been involved in the plot against his life. This particular Falangist had been sent down to Seville under guard and Queipo de Llano had been invited to arrange for his execution. Instead he was imprisoned and some years later the reprieved Falangist, who had been given an important Government job, met Queipo de Llano on the occasion of celebrations in Malaga. The Falangist was heard rather sheepishly to express his gratitude to De Llano for sparing his life. To which the general replied, "Oh, when I told you I'd have you shot you burst into tears. It's so rare in Spain to see a grown man cry that I felt you ought to be kept alive as a museum piece."

The representative of one of our papers, whom I met in Seville, asked me if I would mind vetting an article which he had written on the Easter Week ceremonies. It began, "During Easter Week the priests in Seville say Mass daily."

"Is that O.K.?" he asked.

"Oh yes, it's O.K., but you should add that during Easter Week the priests in Seville have breakfast daily, another of these quaint Sevillian customs."

"Do you mean", he asked, "that it is not only in Easter Week that priests say Mass daily?"

I replied that this was indeed one of their peculiar habits.

"O.K., give me back the article and I'll alter it." Which he did, and his article began, "During Easter Week the priests in Seville say Mass daily with quite unusual pomp."

It was not easy for a journalist who did not even know that priests said Mass daily to understand the Spanish Civil War, a war in which the religious issue was of supreme importance. It is only a minority of Englishmen who feel strongly about religion, but in Spain everybody realises that the Church matters. There are very few genuine atheists in Spain. Those who describe themselves as such are more commonly men in revolt against God, Republicans determined to dethrone the King of Kings as a punishment for his mismanagement of the universe.

There is one point on which every Spaniard is agreed, the importance of the Church in the life of the country. He may hate the Church and welcome the first opportunity to kill priests and to burn churches. Alternatively he may love the Church and be ready both to die and to kill if the Church is threatened. He may be anti-clerical and yet realize that the Spanish way of life has its roots in the Faith and fiercely resent any attempt to destroy the Catholic culture, while himself making no attempt to conform to the Catholic code of morals. But even those who describe themselves as Communists or anarchists retain a suspicion that the Church has the key to life in the world to come. Very few of those Reds who were executed for atrocities refused to see a priest before they died.

In 1936 Mr. Peter Kemp came down from Cambridge. The Civil War had just broken out. Peter Kemp realized far more clearly than did most of his countrymen, and I fear than some of our Catholics, what was really at stake in Spain and he decided to enlist as a volunteer to help to save Spain from Communism. He is a man with a taste for adventure. During the Second World War he took part in a number of raids on the coast of Normandy, Brittany and the Channel Islands. In 1943 he was parachuted into Albania, where he organized guerilla warfare, and in 1944 he was parachuted into Poland, where he was duly imprisoned by our noble allies, the Russians, when Poland was "liberated". Shortly before the Japanese surrender he was parachuted into Siam.

Peter Kemp was, in brief, the kind of volunteer who would be properly appreciated in a country in which physical courage is esteemed beyond all other virtues. The Spaniards are indeed absurdly quixotic in their attitude to danger. I do not myself believe that some units at the beginning of the Civil War thought it disgraceful to dig trenches, but whoever invented this story had a just if ironic appreciation of the Spanish attitude. I myself saw a Spaniard leading an attack up a hill held by Republican machine-gunners. He was carrying a large banner to advertise his presence and was of course killed.

I remember a characteristic incident in the course of my wanderings round and near the front. We were on foot at the time and we had to cross a street under fire from the Reds. "In the Alps", I said to my friend, "it is a tradition to run across a gully down which stones are likely to fall. I propose to run across this street. Your tradition, I know, is to expose yourself uselessly to enemy fire, so do not, I beg you, be deterred from strolling across at a leisurely pace. Let each of us respect his own traditions." I ran, and he walked. When we resumed our conversation I congratulated him on his humility.

"What do you mean?" he asked.

"Well," I replied, "I am vain enough to believe that I can be of some service to the Catholic cause in Spain and so I am anxious to remain alive long enough to write a book about your war, but from the slow pace at which you walked across that street it is clear that you do not believe that your disappearance would make any difference to the Nationalists."

Eileen O'Brien, the charming and attractive Irish-American girl who rendered signal services to the Catholic cause in Spain, was once chatting to an officer in the Requetés when the Reds opened up a bombardment and a shell fell within a hundred yards of where they were talking.

"What about taking shelter?" said Eileen. The Requeté officer looked at her with amazement.

"But surely", he said, "you're in a state of grace?"

Only one excuse was regarded as valid for taking shelter, an unconfessed mortal sin.

The Spaniards have the defects of their qualities. They die without fuss and they often kill without compunction. The reputation of the Spaniards for cruelty is, however, not as well founded as is generally supposed. "The Spaniards", said my friend the Infante Alfonso, "are deeply shocked that it should be necessary to have a society for the prevention of cruelty to children in England. No Spaniard would be cruel to a child." As I write one man is on trial in England on a charge of strangling a four-year-old girl, and another on a charge of murdering a small boy. As to bull-fighting, I am inclined to believe that if bulls and hunted foxes and deer compared notes in the animals' paradise there would be little support for the English view that Spanish blood sports are more cruel than ours.

The Spaniard, however, is often insensitive to pain, his own as well as other people's, and is apt to be ruthless in war. Prisoners were freely killed on both sides in the Civil War, but only the Reds *tortured* prisoners. Neither side was inclined to spare the foreigner who had intervened in a

Spanish quarrel, and one of the most poignant passages in all war literature is the description in Peter Kemp's book of the English volunteer in the International Brigade. It is to the credit of General Franco that he sternly discouraged the shooting of prisoners and in the later phases of the war such deplorable incidents were uncommon.

In 1938 I learned that many British members of the International Brigade were in prison at Lerida. My book *Spanish Rehearsal* had been published and been well received in Spain and it occurred to me that if I applied for permission to see them it could not do any harm and might perhaps prove helpful. The grape-vine had been busy before I arrived, for the fact that I was coming was known to the prisoners, and as I entered the large room where they were awaiting me I saw one of them being bundled out of the room by two guards with bayonets ready to give a helpful prod if necessary.

"They want to stop me seeing you", shouted the prisoner, and I recognized the authentic note of fear in his voice.

The prisoner in question, an Irishman, was under sentence of death. He had, so his fellow-prisoners told me, been accused of running amuck and murdering civilians when the Reds captured Teruel. I wrote personally to General Franco to intercede on his behalf and I learned later that he had been reprieved.

I have seldom met a more disconsolate group of men than these members of the International Brigade. They were thoroughly disillusioned. The Reds, they complained, always thrust the International Brigade into the forefront of the battle and failed to give them adequate support. It is a tradition in Spain heartily to dislike any foreign allies who intervene in Spanish wars, irrespective of whether they are on your side or the enemy's. The kind of complaints made by the International Brigade would have been endorsed by many Irishmen on the Catholic side.

Among the prisoners were two naval ratings who had gone ashore at Malaga and after a drunken debauch woke up to find themselves in gaol. They were offered the alternative of joining the International Brigade or remaining in gaol.

There was one prisoner who had every cause for alarm. General Franco had released many prisoners and allowed them to return to England on giving an undertaking not to rejoin the Brigade. One of these prisoners had returned to Red Spain, rejoined the Brigade and been captured. It was, of course, grossly dishonourable to break his word, but however much one might condemn him for this one could not help admiring his courage in returning to that hell. He was, of course, fighting under a different name but his friends were naturally anxious. So far as I know he was never identified as a returned prisoner who had broken his parole.

Peter Kemp writes as well as he fights. In all the literature of the war there are few books better written than *Mine Were of Trouble*. His faith in the cause for which he fought was unshaken by the occasional relapses into savagery which he witnessed, and the clarity with which he recognizes the defects of the Spanish character is matched by his whole-hearted admiration for the courage, self-sacrifice and chivalry of the Spanish soldier at his best. As for instance this moving story of a Requeté officer.

> Soon the hospital filled with wounded from the Ebro. A young Requeté officer from Navarre with a mangled leg was brought into my room. He was in terrible pain, his face green and waxy with sweat. Unlike me, he never complained of his wound, but expressed himself delighted to be sharing a room with an Englishman who had come to fight for the cause of Spain. I woke up one day after a long period of oblivion to find that he had gone. Eileen O'Brien told me the reason: the hospital

was overcrowded, with fresh casualties pouring in; one of us two had to be moved to another hospital further away. I was unconscious when the order came, but the Requeté contended that, as an English volunteer, I must have priority over him; although he was in no better state than I to travel, he insisted on going. Deeply moved, I begged Eileen to find him and thank him for me. She shook her head:

"I can't. He died on the way."

Peter Kemp, a Protestant, was one of the very few English volunteers on the Catholic side in Spain. All the thirty thousand Portuguese were volunteers; six thousand of them were casualties. The Infante said that they had fought magnificently. Of the Italians who fought in Spain about a third were volunteers. General O'Duffy recruited an Irish Battalion to fight in Spain but they did not stay long.

It is only fair to add that when the Irish eventually went into action, in the Valdemoro-Ciempozuelos sector, the Spaniards were filled with admiration for the bearing and courage of the troops. Indeed, the quality of the men was superb. They were truly inspired with the ideal of fighting for their faith. With good leadership they could have been worthy successors of the famous Corps that fought for France in the eighteenth century:

On mountain and field from Berlin to Belgrade
Lie the soldiers and chiefs of the Irish Brigade.

But they had no chance with the leadership O'Duffy gave them. Quarrels with the Spanish became more frequent and more bitter. In the summer of 1937 the Irish Brigade went home.

Peter Kemp pays a tribute to a Catholic Englishwoman, Gabrielle Herbert, who ran her own hospital in the Huesca sector of the Aragon front.

> Huesca was invested on three sides by the enemy, and Miss Herbert's hospital was under direct fire from enemy artillery for several months.

Many of those who fought in the Italian Brigade were genuine volunteers and some of them had volunteered to save the Church in Spain from the Communists.

It is not easy to understand why the Catholics of the English-speaking world were, with the exception of the Irish, unrepresented in Spain, whereas hundreds of British and Americans, including some gallant idealists from our universities, fought in the International Brigade. It is not as if Catholics were more reluctant than other people to risk their lives in a good cause. The exact reverse is the case. Catholics were over-represented in the fighting forces during the Second World War and an exceptional number of Catholics received rewards for gallantry. I suspect that our reluctance to involve ourselves in foreign wars is partly due to the fact that we have been conditioned to react against the charge that we are less patriotic than Protestants because we suffer from a divided allegiance, to the Queen and to the Pope. Where our country is involved in war the Catholics rush to the colours but we do not join crusades in foreign countries.

We Catholics are less homogeneous than the Jews when our co-religionists are being persecuted. Admittedly the Catholic support for the Catholic cause in Spain was all but unanimous. When Mr. Roosevelt was proposing to lend-lease arms to Red Spain thousands of American Catholics protested to the White House and the arms were not sent. Mr. Chamberlain told a friend of mine that if it had not been for the Catholics in England he might have been forced to blockade Nationalist Spain.

There was however an important minority of Catholics who did nothing to help our efforts. I have an immense admiration for M. Maritain. On the rare occasions when we met I was captured by his charm, and I owe a great debt to his books, but I was saddened by his attitude during the Civil War. His neutralist attitude had a considerable effect on the lay professors in many of the American Catholic Universities, notably Notre Dame, where I worked as a visiting professor during the Michaelmas terms of 1936–8.

Maritain is a philosopher and was much exercised as to how the Nationalist cause could be described as a crusade. I did not myself care a button how we were described, provided that we won, but my crude approach is very different from that of a subtle philosopher. If I am convinced that one side is 70% in the right, I am 100% behind that side and prefer to postpone all discussion of rights and wrongs until the issue has been decided in our favour. All that interested me was that Catholics were free to worship in Nationalist Spain whereas in Red Spain the churches were burnt or defiled and only the priests who were in hiding escaped being shot.

I met M. Maritain in America in November 1940. He was very depressed because he could make no impression on Catholic isolationists. And this was perhaps not surprising.

"We're prepared to provide *you* with a platform," an American priest said to me in 1940, "because when you say that Hitler is an enemy of the Faith we know that you are not merely making yourself the mouthpiece of British propaganda. During the Spanish Civil War you defended the Catholic cause in spite of the fact that so many of your countrymen thought it unpatriotic to align yourself with a cause supported by Hitler and Mussolini. Now that France is in danger Maritain has no philosophical doubts about this war. It's a crusade all right. Maritain was upset because the Catholics accepted help from Hitler, but I'm pretty sure that if Russia ever fights on your side Maritain will have no scruples about enlisting the aid of a dictator as evil as Hitler and even more hostile to the Catholic Church."

But though M. Maritain had little influence on the Catholic isolationists, no continental Catholic has had a greater influence on American Protestants, both during and since the war. He was for years on the Faculty of Princeton, and the fact that he was not a whole-hearted partisan of the Catholic cause in Spain no doubt increased his influence in non-Catholic circles. I have mentioned his attitude during this war because it would be impossible to write about the Civil War without some reference to the divisions in our own Catholic ranks, but I hope I have made it clear that my differences from Maritain on that particular issue in no way diminish my great respect for his notable contribution to Catholic philosophy and apologetics.

The Catholic minority who refused to commit themselves to the support of the Catholic cause in Spain, who maintained a neutralist attitude, were not composed solely of Catholics with left or, at least, left-centre views. An occasional Tory took a similar line—my hostess, for instance, at a house where I was invited to spend the night after giving a lecture to raise funds for an ambulance which English Catholics were sending out to the Spanish Nationalists.

I arrived in time for tea. My hostess was an aristocrat by birth and a Catholic by conversion and a particularly insular type of Tory by conviction.

"I don't like the Spaniards," she remarked as she

poured out my tea. I said nothing. "I don't believe in raising money for foreign charities. There are plenty of deserving cases in England."

I did not argue the point, for it would have been useless to explain that the ambulance for which I was trying to collect money could hardly be described as a "foreign charity". It was a token payment to those Catholics in Spain who were dying in a battle which was ours as well as theirs. Further insults to Spain followed and I rose from my seat.

"Will you forgive me if I go up to my room? I've unpacked my bag and I would like to repack it before the lecture as I prefer to motor home tonight."

My hostess was startled but she was too intelligent to ask me why I had changed my mind. She knew. The dinner party was sticky, and my host was obviously perplexed by the low temperature at the other end of the table. I gave my lecture and left immediately afterwards for home.

In Spain the Catholic cause triumphed; in England the Church suffered a slight setback during the Civil War. But Fascism is no longer a threat to our country, and the majority of those who were enthusiastic supporters of the Red cause in Spain are today secretly pleased that Spain is not a Soviet satellite. Our countrymen have been slow to realize the nature of the Communist threat to our way of life, but the revolution in Hungary restored sight to many of the blind.

The fact that the Church from the first predicted the shape of Communist things to come, and that there has been no Catholic equivalent of the Dean of Canterbury, has had some influence on Protestants, many of whom are now prepared to admit that the Catholic Church, alone among Christian communions, has been wholly uninfected by Communism. The "clerico-fascists" line of attack on the Church is a rather moribund "survival" and is in the process of being replaced as I have suggested, by neo-Malthusiasm. It is the Church's teaching on contraception and on divorce which is perhaps destined to be the main issue between Catholics and non-Catholics in the years to come.

IX

"POPULAR CHRISTIANITY"

I HAVE, I hope, convinced the reader that in the twenty-five years since I became a Catholic the secularist attack on the Church has shifted its ground. We hear far less than we did of the alleged conflict between science and religion, or of "clerico-fascism", but the attack on the Church, once timid and half-hearted, for refusing to condone contraception, has gained in vigour. As far as the defence of Catholic claims against Protestants is concerned there has been a change of emphasis, the significance of which is not yet fully appreciated by Catholics and not yet recognized by Protestants. Nearly a century has passed since the infallibility of the Pope was the main issue on which we parted company with those who were not in communion with Rome, but today it is our belief in the infallibility of Christ which divides us from an increasing number of Protestants. It is, of course, only a minority of Protestants who are even conscious of the fact that they no longer believe in the infallibility of Christ, but the rejection of this belief is implicit in the denial of a basic doctrine of historic Christianity, Christ's own teaching of the possibility of eternal punishment for sinners. There is no place for hell in what Dr. Edward Lyttelton, some time headmaster of Eton, called "Popular Christianity".

A few weeks before I was received into the Church Dr. Lyttelton, the privilege of whose friendship I enjoyed for many years, sent me a copy of his book *Whither?*

in which he described and condemned "Popular Christianity":

> Christ emphasised the peril in which all men live owing to the deceptions practised on them by a spiritual Tempter. . .
>
> It is considered a sign of enlightenment to suppress all mention and all thought of a personal Tempter . . . He habitually spoke of Himself as bringing to men an offer from God which He describes as the offer of Eternal Life.
>
> The ordinary view of the Gospel is that it is a tragic story, attached to which are various beautiful appeals to our sense of duty . . .
>
> All the teaching and the work of Christ imply an inconceivable malignity in sin.
>
> To-day it has been publicly remarked, the modern man does not trouble about his sins.
>
> He [Christ] insisted that the consequences of rejection of God's offer would be unspeakably awful.
>
> Popular Christianity makes no mention of a final Judgment or indeed of Judgment at all. The very conception of a *Dies Irae* is all but extinct.

It is curious that Dr. Lyttelton should have hoped that his book might help me to resist the appeal of Rome, for of course its effect was the precise opposite. The contrast which Dr. Lyttelton drew between traditional and "Popular Christianity" told in favour of the Church which has never been infected by those errors so properly denounced by Dr. Lyttelton. Of these errors none has had a more devastating effect on traditional Christianity than the fact that "Popular Christianity makes no mention of a final judgment", and that the "very conception of a *Dies Irae* is all but extinct".

An obvious result is a new alignment which only approximately corresponds to the division between those Christians who do and those who do not believe in the infallibility of Christ. The decreasing minority of Methodists, for instance, who hold the faith that Wesley held, are far nearer to the Catholic Church than they are to the majority who have implicitly or explicitly discarded John Wesley's belief in eternal punishment. It was this belief which provided the dynamic energy of his evangelical campaigns. He was consumed by a passion for the salvation of souls, and felt that every hour spent on any other purpose was wasted. He could not even forget the judgement during a visit to the British Museum. "Seven huge apartments are filled with curious books," he wrote in his famous *Journal*, "five with manuscripts, two with fossils of all sorts, and the rest with various animals. But what account will a man give to the judge of the quick and the dead for a life spent in collecting all these?"

The differences of belief which separate John Wesley from the Catholic Church are incomparably smaller than those which separate the beliefs of John Wesley from the beliefs of the majority of modern Methodists. Many years ago Dr. Ernest Rattenbury, at that time perhaps the ablest man in the Methodist ministry, remarked to me that Methodism had lost something of its dynamic when Methodists ceased to believe in hell. "There was", he said, "a tremendous drive behind the evangelist who believed that his efforts might save some of those in his congregation from eternal torment. But that drive has gone, and Methodism will find it difficult to discover an adequate substitute."

Cyril Joad, in our published controversy, was taken aback when I reminded him that the doctrine of eternal punishment was not the invention of sadistic priests but was preached by our Lord.

"My remark", wrote Joad, "that Hell is an invention of the priesthood must be withdrawn; it was born of the desire to do what I could by dint of a little harmless omission, for the reputation and memory of one whom I both admire and revere, and I am sorry, for Christ's sake, that you won't let it pass. However, since you insist on it, Christ must have the discredit of authorising Hell . . ."[1]

Joad was writing as an agnostic, but he was the product of a disintegrating Protestantism in which there is no longer any place for a truth to which Christ returned again and again (five times in the Sermon on the Mount alone)—that the unrepentant sinner chooses eternal loss. That Joad should need to be reminded of the elements of Christ's teaching was not unexpected, but that Dr. G. G. Coulton should expose himself to much the same rejoinder was surprising, at least to those who assumed that a scholar who has specialized in medieval Catholicism would correlate what he read with the main sources of Catholic theology, the New Testament. But like Joad he fell into the same error of attacking the Church for what was in effect her fidelity to the teaching of Christ.

"Of course your real quarrel", I wrote, "is not with the Church, but with Christ. Christ was intolerant of error. Christ warned us of the possibility of eternal damnation. St. Thomas, you complain, contrasts the 'few' who shall be saved with the very many 'who shall be damned'. Very intolerant of St. Thomas, almost as intolerant as Christ, who said: 'Wide is the gate, and broad is the way that leadeth to destruction, and many there be which go in thereat: because strait is the gate, and narrow is the way, which leadeth unto life, and few there be that find it.' "[2]

[1] *Is Christianity True?*, p. 149.
[2] *Is the Catholic Church Anti-Social?*, p. 130.

More than twenty of Christ's sayings in the Gospels refer in unambiguous terms to the doctrine of hell. We could not therefore reject the belief in hell without throwing doubt on every saying of our Lord, with the result that the Gospels could no longer be accepted as a divinely inspired guide to life. If on the other hand we accept the record of our Lord's teaching on eternal punishment as correct, and none the less reject that teaching, we must also reject the belief that Jesus was both God and Man, for God could not deceive us and a fallible God is a contradiction in terms.

If Jesus of Nazareth was a holy prophet whose teaching about the next world had no foundation in fact, he might still merit our reverence but not our worship, and those who revere but do not worship Jesus have ceased to be Christians and become Unitarians. Fortunately a man's religious loyalties are not always determined by logic and many of those who do not believe in hell have a great love of our Lord and would be indignant if you denied their right to call themselves Christians. Now whereas there is no Protestant who has any hesitation in proclaiming that he rejects the infallibility of the Pope, most Protestants who reject the belief in hell never face up to the logical consequence of this rejection, the denial that our Lord was infallible. Some of them, indeed, would try to escape from this dilemma by maintaining a theoretical belief in the possibility of a soul's being lost, combined with a secret conviction that this possibility would in fact never be realized. Similarly, I have met Catholics who console themselves with a remark falsely attributed to Cardinal Manning, that hell is a place of eternal torment eternally untenanted. But whatever faint hope Catholics may cherish that the doctrine of eternal punishment is capable of some such interpretation, Catholic teaching and the Catholic way of life are still securely based on unqualified respect for Christ's words and consequently on the belief that this world is an arena where the eternal fate of every individual soul is being decided. Where this belief, the central doctrine of effective Christianity, evaporates, the impoverished Christianity which results is, in effect, a completely different religion.

The Christ of history is replaced by a mixture of Welfare Statesmen and Faith Healer, and Christianity evolves into a religious discipline whose sole object is the good life in this world. Those who still believe in the infallibility of Christ are of course deeply concerned with the improvement of the social order, but the primary though not the only object of their religion is to reach eternal happiness in the world to come.

A group of headmasters had chosen as the subject for discussion: "For what are we preparing our boys?" The chairman, who like most of the headmasters present at this meeting, was a Protestant, turned to the headmaster of Ampleforth and said, "You haven't told us what you are preparing your boys for."

"We prepare our boys for death", was the disconcerting reply. It is, of course, a question of priorities. Ampleforth, like other Catholic schools, prepares its boys both for this world and for the next, and is more successful than most Protestant schools so far as university open scholarships are concerned, but the Catholic school puts first things first. The primary aim of Catholic schools is to reinforce the faith of those who will be exposed to the disintegrating influence of an increasingly secular civilization, and to do all in their power to ensure that their pupils pass the last and most important of all examinations, the examination of death.

By way of contrast let me recall my own education. I was fortunate in that my father and mother were devout Christians, but my father had no real belief in the possibility of a soul's being lost, and my mother, a natural sceptic, was too preoccupied with fighting her own temptations against the Faith to do more than set an example of regular attendance at church. For my father the power of Christ to fortify his own resistance to temptation had been the supreme argument for Christianity.

During the five years which I spent at Harrow I never heard a single sermon which even hinted at the possibility that a soul might be lost. I was prepared for confirmation by my tutor, Sir Arthur Hort, the son of an eminent Anglican divine. That my first duty was to save my soul was never suggested by him or considered by me. Until I was seventeen I said my prayers and considered myself to be a normal Christian, but my values were wholly secular. In so far as Christianity was useful, it was useful in helping me to live a good life and to achieve success. The supreme object of life was fame and posthumous fame. I was immensely ambitious and found it difficult to understand how anybody could be happy who had no hope of fame in this life and no prospect of being remembered for his achievements after death. I worried over the apparent purposelessness of the majority of ordinary lives. This obsession coloured all my thinking and provided a framework of reference for the books which I read. The thought never once crossed my mind that the purpose of life was not fleeting success in this world but the achievement of eternal happiness in the world to come. In brief, though I should have described myself as a Christian, the motives which determined my conduct were wholly secular.

Fortunately my desire for fame weakened as the years passed and as all hope of achieving my youthful ambitions faded. I can appreciate the practical advantages of fame to a *living* man but dead men cannot use posthumous fame and I am pretty sure that if I am conscious in purgatory of what is happening on earth I shall have far more pressing preoccupations than to bother about whether I am still remembered as a ski pioneer. I should, of course, be happy to believe that some of my contributions to apologetics might help one or two people to become Catholics, but I realize that the case for the Church has to be stated in every generation to meet new lines of attack, and if I am remembered at all it will be in connection with ski-ing, and a fat lot of good that will do A. L. expiating his sins in purgatory!

A Catholic friend of mine who spent part of the war in Malta was present at the execution of a Maltese. Two brothers had been caught in the process of burgling a house and the younger brother had shot and killed a policeman. Both brothers were condemned to death, for if two criminals plan a felony in the course of which murder is committed by one of them, both are legally guilty of murder.

But this was just what the elder brother could not and would not see. On the morning of his execution four Dominican friars spent an hour in his cell vainly trying to persuade him to make his confession.

"How can God be just", he kept on exclaiming, "if he lets me be hanged for a murder my brother committed?"

"The younger brother", said my Catholic friend, "had already been hanged when the elder brother was brought into the shed. A kindly English warder said, 'Cheer up, old chap. There's nothing to worry about.' 'Nothing to worry about!' screamed the Maltese, and I must say on that point he had my sympathy.

"I was with a rather senior police officer, a kindly man. I suppose he'd have called himself a Protestant. He was obviously rather bewildered by the crowd round the prisoner, the Dominicans pleading with him to make an act of contrition. They wouldn't let the hangman do his job till they'd extracted some sign of penitence from the Maltese. My friend the police officer became increasingly restive.

" 'Why don't they put the poor devil out of his misery?' he exclaimed. I didn't point out that that was precisely what they were trying to do, save the poor devil from eternal misery. He wouldn't have seen the point. He was the kind of Protestant who just hasn't a clue to what Christ taught about the next life. Meanwhile the poor friars were getting desperate. I could hear them pleading with the Maltese and the occasional mutters of my friend: 'I do wish to God they'd get on with it. It's getting on my nerves. Why don't they hang him and have done with it?'

"The hangman had adjusted the noose round the neck of the Maltese and stood there with his hand on the lever waiting to pull it, but the friars wouldn't give in. When they saw that it was useless to continue the argument they just started praying. 'Jesu-Maria . . . Jesu-Maria . . .' And then at last they were rewarded. I heard the prisoner exclaim 'Jesu-Maria', a priest absolved him and the hangman pulled the lever.

" 'Well, thank God *that's* over', said the policeman. All his reactions emphasized the contrast between the Catholic and the humanist attitudes to death, for of course the policeman's Protestantism was more humanist than Christian."

"If you discount the idea of eternal punishment", wrote Father Knox, "and so rob Christianity of its sharp issues and severe outlines, you alter its character radically; *it is no longer the same religion.*"[1]

[1] *Difficulties*, p. 58. Italics mine.

That policeman in Malta who wanted to "put the poor devil out of his misery" no doubt considered himself to be a Christian, but his form of Christianity was not the Christianity of Christ. It was "no longer the same religion".

"The whole of Christianity," Knox continued, "whether in the New Testament, or in the history of those non-Catholic sects which have preserved a virile tradition of piety, is always framed against a background of finality, of despairing urgency, of claims and duties *absolutely* imperative."

I remember a dinner party at which my host, knowing that I rather enjoyed an argument about the Church, opened the ball with some criticisms of Irish Catholicism. He had been struck by the contrast between the big churches and the poor cottages which so often surrounded them in Irish villages. Well, the pound of ointment with which Mary anointed the feet of Jesus was, we are told, "very costly", and it was Judas who said, "Why was not this ointment sold for three hundred pence and given to the poor?" The Irish poor, like Mary, have often made great sacrifices to do honour to Christ.

A colonel who was present said, "I know nothing about Irish priests in Ireland but the Catholic chaplain in my battalion was an Irishman. He was of peasant origin, I suppose, but he was at home in any company, and what is more he was always up in the front line, crawling about under shell fire to give the sacraments to the dying."

"Yes," said another guest, a major, "I've not much use for the Roman Catholic Church but everybody in the war agreed that the Catholic chaplains were first-class. They were always in the front when there was trouble."

An infantryman is not necessarily braver than a staff

officer because his duty is to fight in the front line, and Catholic chaplains were not braver than Protestant chaplains, but the nature of the work inevitably involved front-line duties. If you don't believe that the Last Sacraments may make all the difference to a sinner why should you crawl about under shell fire to render this service to a dying man? But if life at the front, as elsewhere, is seen "against a background of finality, of despairing urgency", you have no option but to make yourself available to all who are facing eternity.

The Church will, of course, never admit that Christ may have been mistaken in his eschatology, but there is room for great differences of opinion as to the *nature* of eternal punishment. Fifteen years before I became a Catholic I picked up a Catholic Truth Society pamphlet on hell which probably postponed my conversion for many years. The present pamphlet would have been far less dissuasive, for there is an increasing tendency not to go beyond what has been dogmatically defined. We know that hell is the loss of the Beatific Vision, and that surely is enough ground for not wanting to go there.

I have no doubt that what I wrote on this point in *Now I See* would have been thought, if not heretical, at least "theologically rash" a hundred years ago, but as I have said, an exact Italian translation of *Now I See* received the *Imprimatur* in Rome. I certainly could not have become a Catholic if I had been forced to accept as *de fide* the highly-coloured and to my mind repulsive views of the torments of hell which Joad quoted in our correspondence from Catholics writing in an older and vanishing tradition.

X

A RIVEDER LE STELLE

My father never ceased to be a Methodist and was on the roll of Methodist local preachers when he died, but he was confirmed in the Church of England so that he could communicate in the Anglican Church, and his beliefs became increasingly sacramental. His courageous championship of the Catholic cause in Spain during the Civil War brought him increasingly into contact with Catholics and he was not very far from the Church when he died. In his book *The Secret of the Saints* he hoped to do something to encourage the development of the devotional life among Protestants. Long after he lost control of the business which he had founded he retained control of the Hellenic Travellers' Club cruises and it was on one of those cruises that he was stricken down by an illness from which he never recovered. My mother knew that he would be happiest in a Catholic hospital, so she telegraphed to St. John and St. Elizabeth's, and the last words which he spoke were to the Catholic nurse who met him at Dover: "Are you a Roman Catholic?"

"Yes," said the nurse.

"Good," said my father.

He lived until he had been carried into a bedroom next to the chapel in which the Sacrament was reserved, and died with three Catholics kneeling beside his bed. My son, Peter, who had followed me into the Church, was with his grandfather on this cruise and he was faintly dismayed that my father exhibited no desire for spiritual consolation. His only reaction to the Methodist minister whom Peter sent for was a faint sign of recognition, and his lack of interest in the few embarrassed remarks which the minister addressed to him was so marked that he did not come again.

> Such harmony is in immortal minds
> But when the muddy vesture of decay
> Doth grossly close it in we cannot hear it . . .

and in the last days of his life the muddy vesture had all but silenced the immortal harmonies. My father had travelled a long way from the Methodism of his youth but even if he had been in spiritual rapport with the Methodist minister, he was too exhausted to have benefited by spiritual consolation.

A professional has been defined as a man who can do a thing when he is not in the mood to do it and an amateur as a man who can't do it when he is. In the chamber of death the priest is a professional with a job to do which he can do whether or not he or the dying man is feeling particularly spiritual. To the dying Catholic what matters are the Last Sacraments even if these be administered by a priest for whom he has no particular respect.

"I do not think", I said to my son, "that a Catholic who was as near death as your grandfather would have felt any more spiritual than he did, or shown any greater desire for spiritual as opposed to sacramental consolation, but even if he were barely conscious he would react instinctively to the presence of a priest in the room. If he could speak at all he would force himself to articulate a phrase or two to express contrition, *confiteor* or *mea culpa*, and if he could not speak he would indicate contrition and the desire for absolution by a gesture."

It is in general satisfactory to be proved right by subsequent events, but I would have gladly foregone an experience with which I could have reinforced my argument.

E quindi uscimmo a riveder le stelle.
And so we emerged to behold once more the stars.
(The last line of Dante's *Inferno.*)

On a February morning in 1953 I went ski-ing from Mürren with a young married couple, Julian and Brigid Salmond. Julian is the nephew of the Grenfell brothers, who belonged to that tragic group of Balliol men all of whom fell in the First World War. I had been startled to discover that they had chosen for their first mountain, on their honeymoon, the Dent du Géant, one of the steepest of the Chamonix Aiguilles, and had successfully persuaded a guide to take them up this difficult peak without a second guide or porter.

The snow on that day at Mürren was perfect, easy and not too fast, and I thought it would be fun to put what was, perhaps, the first track down beside the newly opened ski-lift. I held this *schuss* without great difficulty, as did Brigid Salmond. On my third run I suddenly decided to put a straight track down the other side of the ski-lift. I ran a steepish slope straight without a preliminary exploration of the ground, and I approached a blind edge at high speed. In fact I broke the rules which I have defined in print for the benefit of other people.

I saw the blind edge, decided to chance it, shot into the air and fell into a ditch formed by a summer stream. There was a vertical drop of about four or five feet into the ditch, which had been masked by drifted snow. I landed on my head, having performed a semi-somersault in the air, and my head drove through a foot or so of powder snow into the compacted crusted snow below. Some of the loose snow from the top of the bank seems to have been swept off as I fell and piled on top of the snow through which I had fallen.

My body sloped downwards, my head three feet or more below the surface, my knees more loosely covered. My right hand, which was extended forwards, was just clear of the snow, but it must have been numbed by the pressure of the snow for it was without sensation.

I remember scooping out a hole above my face so as to let in some air through the crust from the more porous snow above, and I remember continuing this scooping movement until I was rescued, but Julian Salmond assures me that I could not possibly have moved either my right arm, which he dug out with some difficulty from compacted snow, or my left arm, which was twisted and trapped below my body. My recollections therefore must be a mixture of actuality and nightmare in which I confused what I desperately wanted to do with what I succeeded in doing.

I remembered what I had myself written about avalanches, how men can live for hours or, alternatively, die in a few minutes, life or sudden death being determined by the texture of the snow and the position of the body.

Philip Gosset's story of his survival in the avalanche which killed the great Swiss guide, Bennen, in 1863 was familiar to me. Fragments came back to my memory . . . "I saw a faint glimmer of light. The crust above my head was getting thinner." But the crust above my head was getting no thinner. It was with the utmost difficulty that I could free my mouth from the smother of snow. I spat out the snow and I spat out my teeth, and I sucked in what little oxygen remained.

I knew that some little time would pass before I was missed. The Salmonds might think that I had forgotten them and taken the next ski-hoist to the top. Doreen Elliott was shepherding a party of novices. She was looking after them and had no reason to worry about me. Twenty minutes or more might pass before I was dug out. Could I last twenty minutes?

Was it really conceivable, I found myself asking, that I could perish in so absurd a fashion? I had survived so many hazards among the mountains, and so often missed death by inches. Had I been spared the dignity of death among the sovereign heights to die on a snow slope crowded with ski novices, less than five hundred feet above the Palace Hotel, Mürren? Could there be a more humiliating finale to a mountaineering career? This was like drowning in two feet of water.

I know now exactly what Whymper, who had survived unscathed from many mountain perils, must have felt when he walked off the platform on which he had been lecturing about the Matterhorn, and broke his leg.

I soon lost the power of connected thought and passed into a dreamlike existence which I remember much as one remembers a nightmare, not a violent nightmare but a deep depression, a shapeless melancholy.

I knew beyond all possible doubt that I was dying. This was death. How strange that this should be the end. Within a few score yards there were friends who would rush to help me if they knew, if they only knew . . . but the powers that decide these things were determined that they should not know . . .

I continued feebly to spit out the snow from my mouth, and when I felt my consciousness ebbing I spat out a *Confiteor* with the snow, and if God wouldn't take the rest as read (or said) there was nothing more that I could do about it. There was no margin left for any mental or physical effort other than those dedicated to this grim struggle for oxygen. I felt no fear of death and no curiosity as to what would follow death. I was too exhausted either to rebel against fate or to acquiesce in what I dimly felt to be the judgement of heaven. It was useless to pray, for this must have been designed. In all recorded ski-ing history, which none knew better than I, there was not one single case of a skier being suffocated by snow as the result not of an avalanche but of a fall. I could have fallen into that ditch a thousand times and scrambled out unhurt. And the more clouded my mind, the greater the confusion between the beliefs I have come to hold and the outcrop of things read in my youth, such as Greek plays in which vindictive deities imposed ruthless penalties for pride. I remembered the *hubris* with which I had taken the slope straight . . . *Di me terrent et Jupiter hostis.*

The one thread of thought which seemed to hold together the blurred images which floated through what was left of my mind was poignant anxiety about my wife and the consequences for her of my folly. Somewhere on the slope Doreen Elliott and Phyllis Holt-Needham were ski-ing, and they would have the task of telling her, and in a dim grey fashion I felt sorry for them.

Every moment it was becoming more difficult to keep the snow from my mouth, more of an effort to fight for breath and more tempting to surrender, but though I had abandoned hope, I vaguely felt that decency demanded that the last rearguard action against death should be fought as stubbornly as possible. But if I was not actually unconscious, I was only just conscious when I felt a sudden tug as if my ski were being wrenched off my feet . . .

And this is what had happened since I fell. At the moment that I landed in the ditch, a skier was just attaching himself to the moving anchor of the ski-hoist. I do not know or wish to know his name or his nationality but I am glad to know that he was not an Englishman. He saw the accident, as he afterwards admitted, and on his upward journey passed within two yards of the ditch in which I was being slowly suffocated, saw my ski sticking out of the snow, and did not detach himself from the hoist. He had paid for one complete journey to the summit and it would have been a pity to waste his ticket. He did, however, shout a general warning that there was a man on the slope who had had an accident.

Doreen Elliott, who had stopped above a blind edge to warn the inexperienced skiers in her party, hadn't a clue as to who had been hurt or where, for I was invisible from above, but by luck or guidance she reached me without loss of time. She saw my limp hand sticking out of the snow and assumed that I was dead. She shouted for help and began to take off my ski.

Two moments in my life stand out above all others. The first was on a rocky ledge where I lay alone with a leg shattered and blood pouring out of my thigh and arms. For twenty minutes I called in vain for help, and then—at last—I heard an answering shout. The second moment was when I was jerked back into consciousness by the tug on my ski.

That jerk was like an injection to a dying man. Hope flooded back into the all but airless prison in which I was suffocating. Every reserve of physical and mental effort was thrown into the struggle for survival. They tell me that they reached me within five minutes of my fall and that the digging process took two or three minutes. They were long enough, those last three minutes.

One of the first to arrive was Brigid Salmond. My

body was lying crooked, and she began to dig in the wrong place, and suddenly she felt that she saw something moving below the snow. I was far too deeply buried for my slight feeble movements to be visible on the surface, but what scientists call extra-sensory perception is now an established fact, and what is certain is that she started digging in a new place and went straight down to my head. I was so firmly embedded in that crust that she had to tear with her nails to uncover my head.

I had heard nothing of Doreen's shouts for help, but suddenly I heard a faint far-off scratching sound above my head, and a feeling as of a weight being gradually removed. The snow was no longer pressing me in so relentlessly. Air seemed to be filtering in through the lighter snow and then . . . and then . . . I felt fingers on my face and looked up and saw

> that little tent of blue
> Which prisoners call the sky

and there was a rush of air to my mouth and I drank in the life-giving air as if it had been wine, and there were hands below lifting me up, and above the blue sky full of space and freedom, and all shot through with security and gladness.

Fortunately among the rescuers there was a trained nurse and a doctor, Dr. A. E. Flatt. I dimly remember my hands being massaged to restore the circulation. Dr. Flatt tells me that my knees were doubled up against my body and that this aggravated the difficulties of breathing. I was incoherent when I came to the surface. "Medically but not socially conscious", a nice distinction. "You were very blue about the lips and wouldn't have lasted much longer. That girl did a splendid job. She did not waste a moment getting to your head."

Three weeks after my accident the roof of a station at the bottom of a ski-lift in another Alpine centre discharged its snow which avalanched on to a group of waiting skiers. They were all dug out in two or three minutes, but a boy of sixteen was unconscious and died while they were applying artificial respiration.

That poor boy was the victim of an accident for which others were responsible, for the snow should have been removed from the roof before it became dangerous. I, on the other hand, had asked for trouble, and was justly punished for the senile vanity of trying to pretend that I was as young as I felt. I remember murmuring to myself as I reached the bottom of the first run beside the ski-lift, "Pretty good for an old boy in his middle sixties with a game leg," and what followed was a just but humiliating penalty for snowing off.

This discreditable incident, however, seems to me worth recording if only for the deeper significance that my experience has given to the "Hail Mary". "Pray for us sinners now and *in the hour of our death*", for in the hour of our death we may be unable to pray for ourselves.

XI

AN ALPINE TRAGEDY

IN THE story which follows I have altered the names but nothing else. It is an accurate transcript of events which the good burghers of Lindenalp interpreted as the judgement of God.

Long before I met Stephan I knew of him as a distinguished mountaineer with some outstanding pioneer ascents to his credit. He was a rich industrialist, and a genial host. Many a pleasant hour have I spent in the comfortable chalet which he built in the valley which he loved, and which was his home during his declining years. Stephan's wife died when he was in his early fifties and he never remarried. During his last years his house was managed by an Austrian whom I will call Pyrrha because she reminded me of the Pyrrha to whom Horace wrote an ode. She was part housekeeper and part nurse to the ageing Stephan. Pyrrha had been born near the eastern frontiers of the old Austrian Empire and she had far more Slav than Teutonic blood in her veins.

The villagers detested Pyrrha. They were fond of Stephan and resented the manner in which Pyrrha seemed to shut him off from his old friends in the village. Pyrrha, so they felt, was a gold digger, and their dislike of her was intensified when she cast her spells on one of the finest guides in the village, whom we may call Hans, though that was not his name. Pyrrha herself was an ardent climber and particularly good on rocks. A young

Austrian, Sigmund, who had obtained temporary employment in the village, was also dazzled by her charms.

Stephan was in his seventies when he died, and his last years were very, very sad. He had never denied himself anything money could buy, but hope was a commodity which he could not acquire by writing a cheque. He had no religion and no hope of a life beyond the grave.

One of the first things which I did whenever I visited Lindenalp was to ring up Stephan, and shortly before his death I telephoned to his chalet. Pyrrha answered the telephone, and asked me to hold the line. After a pause she returned.

"I'm very sorry but Herr Stephan does not want to see anybody."

A few days later we met on a little path near his chalet. He was tottering along on Pyrrha's arm. He did not stop, and gave me the barest nod of recognition as we passed. Never have I seen despair more plainly written on a human face. He died, and his ashes were scattered into the mountain river which he loved. And the village waited with curiosity for his will. It was as they feared. Pyrrha had inherited Stephan's lovely mountain home and enough money to live in comfort.

Shortly after the will had been read I met Pyrrha in the village. She had just returned from a difficult climb. We talked mountain shop, and she asked me to tea and suggested that I should bring my wife.

"I won't call on that woman," said my wife. "She is making that nice wife of her favourite guide unhappy, and anyhow she's not the kind of woman I would ever call on."

Her Austrian friend, Sigmund, was in the chalet when I arrived. I made no excuses for my wife, and Pyrrha was too intelligent to comment on the fact that I was alone.

She told me that she and Sigmund were planning a Himalayan expedition. It was clear that the village had not exaggerated the money which Stephan had left her. The talk wandered from the Himalaya to the Alps. Sigmund was an ambitious climber and had designs on some of the classic north walls, Matterhorn and Jorasses.

"But not the Eiger Nordwand," said Pyrrha with a laugh. "It would be silly to risk one's life on that murderous cliff when the world is just full of mountains which I hope to climb."

How I envied them! They were young, and could look forward to year after year of mountain adventure, but I had climbed my last peak.

I was wrong on both counts. It was Pyrrha and Sigmund who had climbed their last peak but I had not. A few years after this tea party I climbed the Aiguille du Goûter in my sixty-eighth year. And it was not a "murderous cliff" like the Eiger Nordwand but on the ascent of an easy mountain that they died. Sigmund had slipped on an easy icy slope and dragged Pyrrha and Hans with him. The slope, which was not particularly steep, petered out gradually on to the horizontal, and they would have slid to rest and escaped with a few scars and scratches but for a shallow ice ridge which ran across the slope, a ridge which at the worst would have bruised them or perhaps broken a bone had not all three of them struck this ridge with their heads. They were fantastically unlucky, but were they really unlucky? The village thought otherwise. That so expert a party should *all* have been killed on so easy a slope seemed to the villagers clear proof of divine judgement.

On the day after the bodies had been brought down to the valley I met a friend of Pyrrha's in the village who suggested that I might spare a few minutes to look in at the room in the chalet in which Pyrrha was awaiting burial. My wife and I entered the chamber of death, knelt together and said some prayers for poor Pyrrha. I found myself wondering whether Pyrrha had made an act of contrition during those last few seconds of her life as she slid down that ice slope to her death.

As we left the chalet my wife murmured, "Well, she made me call on her after all."

Sigmund's body was taken back to his native Austria, but Pyrrha and the guide Hans are buried in the Lindenalp churchyard. I was present when they were buried. The Protestant *Pfarrer* spoke for about twenty minutes and he said all that he was expected to say, and nothing that a layman could not have said with equal appropriateness. There was no room in his impoverished form of Christianity for purgatory, and no belief in the power of prayer to help the dead, so he paid a tribute to the guide as a great mountaineer, expressed sympathy with his widow and children, murmured something about the unpredictability of life, so that even the best mountaineer could never be certain that he would not return to the valley on a stretcher, and wound up with a little vague religiosity.

We then moved over to that corner of the churchyard in which Catholics are buried. "We all knew," said the priest, "the gossip about this unfortunate woman. Like the rest of us she was a mixture of good and evil, but what encourages me to hope for her salvation was her great love of the mountains. However self-indulgent a mountaineer may be on the plains, he cannot become an expert without self-conquest, for mountaineering is no sport for the soft. This woman was not only an expert climber but she really loved the mountains for their beauty and we can surely hope that among the mountains her heart often went out to the God who made them. She has now gone where gossip can neither harm nor reach her, but our prayers can reach her. She is in need, in desperate need of your prayers, so please stop gossiping about her and start praying for her. Pray that God in his infinite mercy may save her soul . . ."

I walked back through the village with Heinrich, a Swiss friend of mine. "That poor *Pfarrer*," he began, "he had nothing to say. A nice, good man, but really I did not feel he said anything that I could not have said. He was like a man groping in the dark for something on which to hang his beliefs . . . I am a Protestant but the *Pfarrer* had no message for me. What a contrast to the priest! What a sense of reality there was in those few words the priest said! He really knew what he believed and why he believed, and he was so precise about what he wanted us to do for that poor woman. When he demanded we should pray for her one felt that he really believed that prayers might make all the difference to poor Pyrrha. A big difference. Yes, he believed that. He did really . . ."

Heinrich's surprise that a Catholic priest should not only believe but act with conviction on the beliefs which he professed was perhaps disingenuous but also disconcerting as evidence of how far continental Protestantism has travelled from primitive Christianity.

XII

THE TWO INTERNATIONALS

JUDGED by the criterion of material strength there are only two first-class powers in the modern world, the United States and Soviet Russia, but in the battle for the souls of men two great Internationals face each other, the Catholic International based on Rome and the Communist International based on Moscow. And just as Communists can count with confidence on the support of many who do not describe themselves as such, so there should be, and sometimes is, a close co-operation between Catholics and Protestants when faced by the common threat of militant Communism. Nowhere, for instance, are relations between Catholics and Protestants closer than in Eastern Germany.

Whereas Protestants are often wooed by Communism, with rare if sensational successes, the Communists pay the Church the compliment of relentless persecution of Catholics in their power, and implacable hostility to the Church in countries where the Communists are still in a minority. In Soviet Russia, though priests of the Russian Orthodox Church and Baptist ministers are not actively persecuted, only one Catholic priest is permitted to officiate in all Soviet Russia, the priest who officiates in the chapel in Moscow attended by members of the diplomatic corps.

If I were a Communist I should feel very hopeful about the future. In 1957, as the result of democratic and free elections, the Communists gained control of the Indian state of Kerala, of British Guiana, and Naha, the capital city of Okinawa, key to the defence chain of islands which America has organized in the Pacific. In Java the Communists emerged as the largest party and in the Middle East the Communist infiltration has not yet been, and perhaps cannot be, checked.

We are in no danger of ignoring the many secular reasons for Communist success, but we are less anxious, as Christians, to admit that we ourselves are partly to blame. It is only a minority of Christians who act as if they belonged to a Church militant. Most Christians would feel happier in a Church dormant. The average Christian makes a great virtue of keeping his religion and his secular life in separate compartments. There is no such division in the mind of the Communist. The Communist code is binding on Communists in politics, in business, in trade unions and in sport. The Communist trade unionist, for instance, is not concerned to elect the most competent candidate for an important post in his union; his job is to ensure the election of the candidate who is either a Communist or who is under Communist control, in some cases as the result of weakness which exposes him to blackmailing pressure. The Communists are among the first to arrive and the last to leave a trade union meeting, and many a proposal has been rushed through at the end of a meeting because the opposition had gone home to bed. A Communist minority has often secured virtual control of a union as the result of the apathy of the majority; Catholics have often been turned out of key positions in unions in which the Catholics greatly outnumber the Communists.

Every Communist is an ardent propagandist and misses no chance of subversive propaganda, but the overwhelming majority of Christians, Catholic or Protestant, are both incompetent and unwilling to defend their faith. It is only the exceptional layman who feels any obligation to master the case for Christianity and the technique of encouraging non-Christians to discuss their objections to the Faith. Most Christians feel that it is best to leave apologetics to specialists, clerical or lay. Admittedly, one must take some time off from television to equip oneself to help people searching for the truth, and it is only too easy to rationalize one's reluctance to qualify as a lay apologist by some such formulæ as, "It does no good to thrust one's views on other people", or, "Nobody is ever converted by argument", or, "The only way to make converts is to set a good example".

The Apostles certainly did no good to *themselves* by "thrusting their views on other people", but there would have been no early Church if Christians had not obeyed our Lord's command to go into the world and preach the Gospel to every creature, including creatures who were quite violent in their reaction to those who may be generically described as view-thrusters. I am, however, prepared to admit that view-thrusting is a special vocation and that every Christian is not called to the life of a missionary at home or abroad. All I claim is that a Christian who has equipped himself by study to meet the ordinary objections to the Faith and to help an honest inquirer searching for the truth is of rather more value than a Christian who is painfully embarrassed by any discussion of his religion with those who do not share it.

It is true that nobody is ever *wholly* converted by argument, but rational argument has been an important factor in many conversions, my own among them. I should be the last to belittle the persuasive power of a saintly or near-saintly life, but realizing rather sadly that my own example would have, if anything, a dissuasive effect on potential converts I have done my best to master the easier alternative, the attempt to convert people by argument.

If one party in a General Election canvassed with zeal and the other party refused to canvass on the ground that nobody was ever converted by argument, and that the only way to win voters was to set a good example, one would not need to be an expert Gallup pollster to forecast which party would win the election.

It is only in moments of acute crisis that the Catholic laity as a whole can be aroused to take effective action against Communism. The Communists, through agents who of course described themselves as Socialists, all but secured effective control of Spain when Catholic Spain rose in armed revolt, and it is more than probable that the Communists and their allies, the Nenni Socialists, would have won the critical 1948 election in Italy but for the campaign brilliantly organized by the militants of "Catholic Action". In less critical times the majority of Christians contribute nothing to the defence of the Faith and are apparently undismayed by the contrast with the armies of Communism, every soldier in which is dedicated to the destruction of Christendom.

XIII

THE PROBLEM OF CONTACT

My subject was "Europe from a Catholic Angle" but the lady who was responsible for the notice of my lecture in Copenhagen had an imperfect knowledge of English, with the result that I learned from the typewritten notice that the Copenhagen Catholics were to enjoy the privilege of a lecture on "Europe by a Catholic Angel". And I suppose if a real angel had given the lecture there might have been a few hundred Protestants in the audience, but lacking this attraction the lecture ran true to what I can only call the "catacomb" type, my audience consisting almost exclusively of Catholics.

Since I became a Catholic I have given nearly a thousand lectures in all five continents and I should be sorry to believe that the effort involved was wholly wasted. I can at least hope to have provided some Catholics with ammunition to use in friendly arguments with sceptics, but the unconverted whom I would welcome on such occasions seldom attend lectures held under Catholic auspices. On the other hand the unconverted turn up in great numbers to a debate. I have lectured more often than I can remember to Newman Societies in British, American, Canadian and Australian universities. The average attendance varies from about one hundred to two hundred, and is almost exclusively Catholic, but when the Newman Club in Melbourne University arranged a debate for me with the secretary of the Australian Rationalist Society a big hall was packed, and people of whom only a minority were Catholics were standing four deep at the back throughout the two hours' debate. The event was so popular that we had to have a repeat performance in Melbourne itself.

The contact problem applies not only to the unconverted but also to the lukewarm Catholic and to the Catholic who has ceased, or who is about to cease, practising. Such Catholics do not attend lectures under Catholic auspices but will often come to a debate. I remember being much cheered by a letter which I received from a Catholic after a debate with an atheist in London. My correspondent wrote that he had been on the point of leaving the Church and had come to the debate expecting that I would get much the worst of the argument, but that as a result of the debate he was returning to the practice of his religion. If this had been the sum total of what I have achieved by debating I should not feel that I had wasted my time.

Debating seems to me one of the more effective ways in which to reach those Catholics in our universities who are subjected to steady anti-Catholic and indeed anti-Christian influences. The majority of those who teach in our schools and universities are not even nominal Christians. Logical positivism was until recently the dominant philosophy in the universities of the English-speaking world.

It is characteristic of our modern prophets that they react indignantly if anybody suggests that those who preach moral nihilism may be expected to practise what they preach. Thus Sir Herbert Read can write in his book *Surrealism* (p. 52) of Byron and the Marquis de Sade, "The function of such figures is to be so positive in their immorality that morality becomes negative by comparison. They show, by the more than human energy of their evil, that evil too, as Milton was compelled to admit, has its divinity. In short, they reveal the conventionality of all systems of morality. They prove that the most deeply rooted taboos, such as incest, can be thwarted by the individual will; and the courage they manifest in such defiance is so absolute that a figure like Byron becomes the unconfessed hero of humanity."

When, however, Mr. J. B. Priestley drew attention to the fact that the surrealists include an undue proportion of perverts, Sir Herbert bridled with indignation at this "insult", instead of citing this perversion as welcome evidence that really great men can defy "the most deeply rooted of taboos". Similarly, I should be surprised and faintly disappointed if my suggestion that there is no rational ground on which a logical positivist can condemn the seduction of a pupil by a professor did not provoke shrill protests from any logical positivists who did me the honour of reading what I have just written. I disclaim any intention of implying that logical positivists actually practise the moral nihilism which they preach, but I cannot believe that philosophers can continue indefinitely to insist that a particular code has no rational basis without ultimately undermining the code in question.

Professor A. J. Ayer, a leading exponent of logical positivism, whose book *Language, Truth and Logic* acquired at Oxford, according to *The New Statesman* (26 June 1948), almost "the effect of a philosophic bible", asserted that there are only two types of statement that have meaning, analytical propositions such as $2 \times 3 = 6$, and propositions which can be verified by science and sense-experience.

It follows, to quote the founder of logical positivism, Wittgenstein, that "there can be no ethical proposition", a view which would seem to be endorsed by Wittgenstein's most influential disciple in England, Professor A. J. Ayer. "If I now generalize," he writes, "and say 'stealing is wrong', I produce a sentence which has no factual meaning—that is, expresses no proposition which can be either true or false."[1]

By parity of reasoning we could show that the sentence, "Fornication is wrong," is a "sentence which has no factual meaning", and that the sentence, "It is wrong for a professor of philosophy to seduce one of his own pupils", expresses no proposition "which can be either true or false". "The only way to get rid of temptations", said Oscar Wilde, "is to yield to them." Maybe, but the very word "yielding" is a relic of an old-fashioned vocabulary which has ceased to be relevant now that we have realized that all talk of temptation is meaningless.

Now one of the odd things about so many of these professors who teach what is, in effect, moral nihilism, is that they react indignantly to any suggestion that they or their pupils practise what they preach.

I remember a friendly discussion with a group of logical positivists who were teaching philosophy at an Australian university. They themselves, I was assured by one who knew them, were men of character who lived by a code which on their own theory they should have condemned as meaningless. I raised the question of the mass murder of Jews by Hitler, an embarrassing challenge to the logical positivists, who maintain that all moral judgements are meaningless. Most logical positivists have been vaguely leftist, not of course because they have any particular sympathy with the poor but because Conservatism in politics is associated in their minds with conservative

[1] "Bertrand Russell has told us recently (in the *Hibbert Journal* for last July) that philosophy in its present phase has abandoned the task of interpreting the world, and that it tends to occupy itself with analysing what silly people mean when they say silly things . . . If they [the linguistic analysts] think with that much over-rated philosopher, Ludwig Wittgenstein, that philosophy 'neither explains nor deduces anything' and that the end of philosophy is that 'philosophical problems should completely disappear' (*Philosophical Investigations*), there can be little question of philosophical analysis preparing the way for anything but a cessation of philosophizing." (*The Month*, Jan. 1957.)

morals. Because logical positivists are usually leftists they would not be embarrassed if challenged to reconcile their philosophy with such statements as "it is wrong for Communists to murder Catholic priests", because in progressive circles there is a tendency to agree with the author of a book on the Civil War in Spain that "martyrdom is a professional risk for a Spanish priest", and that "since civil war is a category of politics it is reasonable that a man should be liquidated for his opinions". But the mere fact of being a Jew cannot be classified as a legitimate professional risk, and Professor A. J. Ayer, who, of course, feels strongly on anti-Semitism, was finally forced to revise his philosophy in order to allow for moral judgements condemning Hitler's liquidation of the Jews. It was amusing to watch the embarrassment of his Australian disciples when challenged on this issue.

Towards the end of my discussion with the Australian philosophers I asked them what meaning a logical positivist could attribute to philosophy itself. In the past, philosophy had been concerned with the most significant problems which had exercised the minds of men, with the existence of God, the objective basis of morality, the meaning of the universe and the purpose of life, but all such speculations are relegated by the logical positivists to the status of propositions which are neither true nor false but merely meaningless. My friends agreed that philosophy was meaningless. "Why then", I asked, "should universities continue to pay salaries to philosophers who themselves admit that philosophy is meaningless?" Nobody was quick enough to reply, "Your implied moral judgement 'It is wrong to accept a salary and give nothing in return' is as meaningless as the statement 'stealing is wrong'."

Fashions in sophistry change very rapidly, and it is no longer fashionable to describe oneself as a logical positivist.

I have discussed logical positivism at some length because the fact that it survived as long as it did proves that we have not yet solved the problem of contact with modern sophists and their dupes, for there was never in all the long history of philosophic error a more egregious example of an untenable philosophy than logical positivism. According to Dr. Eric Unger, Professor Ayer's originality consisted in the fact that no philosopher had been more "outspoken in his denial of the possibility of any moral knowledge", but there is nothing particularly praiseworthy in the originality which consists in expounding views too foolish ever to have been anticipated by all the sophists of the past. What finally killed logical positivism was the fact that every logical positivist was forced to admit some moral judgements were far from meaningless.

Professor Ayer did in point of fact debate with Father Martin D'Arcy, S.J., on the B.B.C. and with Father Thomas Corbishley, S.J., at Oxford, experiences which he was naturally not in a hurry to repeat, but far too few people ever heard of these debates.

I believe that the problem of contact could be partially solved if we faced the fact that the only way to produce effective apologists is by the method of debate. We should begin by trying to arrange discussions or debates between young Catholics and young Protestants or Communists. A debate between the Young Catholic Workers and the Young Communist League in the north of England in 1944 resulted in a shattering defeat for the Communists. One can only learn to box by boxing, to debate by debating, and inevitably the young Catholic champions would begin by making many mistakes for which they would be duly jeered at by their youthful supporters, and thereby stimulated, as no schoolmaster could stimulate them, to improve their debating technique.

The school and the university should be regarded as

the nursery of Catholic controversialists, the best of whom would subsequently be invited to join a society founded to compel our modern sophists to emerge from the classrooms where their mischief cannot be controlled and to defend their sophistries in public debate. The society might well be called "The Society of Catholic Rationalists",[1] for the name and the existence of such a society would do something to educate the academic world in the basic fact of Catholic apologetics. Cyril Joad began our correspondence with the suggestion that he would allow me to play the trump card of faith once and once only. He was plainly disconcerted when I informed him that I had no intention whatever of appealing to authority or to faith in support of my beliefs. The Church has in fact condemned fideism as a heresy, a fideist being defined as a man who denies the power of unaided human reason to reach certitude, and who affirms that the fundamental act of human knowledge consists in an act of faith.

The Society of Catholic Rationalists, if it received ecclesiastical backing, and if membership were regarded as an honour conferred on fully qualified debaters, would soon acquire a status which would make it difficult for sophists to decline "an invitation to public discussion", a formula which seems to me more diplomatic than "a challenge to public debate". The existence of such a society would save Catholics from the humiliation which is the inevitable result of pitting a quick-witted sophist against a Catholic intellectual with no experience of debating.

The Society of Catholic Rationalists would not only promote public debates but would also provide speakers for private and informal discussions. In time the Society would, I hope, have branches in every university and in every big town. A Catholic student who was exasperated

[1] Unless the Catholic Evidence Guild or the Newman Association adds the organization of formal debates to its existing programme.

by the clever sophistries of some atheist professor would then be in a position courteously to suggest an informal discussion either during a class or at some other time convenient to the professor between the professor and a member of the Society of Catholic Rationalists. If the professor declined the class would draw their own conclusions.

At the moment it is easy for the ill-informed denigrators of Christianity to evade exposure of their sophistries. A well-known American publisher, to quote one instance, failed to tempt Mr. Paul Blanshard to collaborate with me in a controversial exchange of letters, but if the challenge were issued by a Society which enjoyed the official support of the Hierarchy, it would be less easy for people to escape from the dialectical arena. No professor can be blamed if he is unwilling to risk exposure in front of his own pupils. In 1952 I had a public debate with Professor Irvin Edman, head of the philosophic faculty at Columbia. Mr. Edman was a humanist with no belief in any form of supernatural religion and the author of some books which seem to have been widely read. Not only was the large hall in which we debated full, but the debate was relayed to a lower hall which was also full. More than half the audience were non-Catholics.

I liked Mr. Edman. He was a friendly man but no debater. He would have had to be an exceptionally able debater to produce a plausible affirmative reply to the question which we were discussing: "Can the values of humanism be preserved without supernatural religion?" I shall never forget a wistful *cri de coeur* which he injected into his last speech. "I do so admire this Oxford way of being mean to you. They can be mean in such a gentlemanly way that nobody knows how mean they're being."

That was in 1952. Since then I have not been able to secure a debate at any university, but if the kind of society which I suggest were already in existence, there would be debates of this type at every university at which Catholics are represented.

If Christianity be true it is infinitely the most important of all truths, and Catholic apologetics should therefore be the foundation of a Catholic education. Unfortunately there is a lack of obvious inducement to master this particular branch of knowledge. Success in other subjects may be rewarded by scholarships on leaving school for the university, or by well-paid appointments on leaving the university for the world, but there are no worldly inducements to encourage young people to master the defence of the Faith. Memory is highly selective and knowledge which is divorced from action, and unrelated to subjects in which the student is genuinely interested, is forgotten all too soon. I can only write of what I know from personal experience but there is much in this chapter which applies equally to Anglicans.

The teaching of apologetics in Catholic schools has a threefold object.

Firstly, to ensure that Catholics are not worried by the direct and indirect attacks on the Faith to which they will be exposed in the world.

Secondly, in the hope that some of those who have studied apologetics at school will be able to help the occasional non-Catholic who is searching for truth to find his way into the Church. Our Catholic schools and colleges can render the Church an immense service by promoting the unostentatious apostolate of those Catholics who never write or speak in public, but who can answer the difficulties raised by non-Catholics in private conversation and who can thus make converts through personal contacts.

Thirdly, to produce an increasing number of apostolic Catholics who are equipped to defend the Faith in books and articles, and by public debate with non-Catholics.

How far are our Catholic schools achieving these objects?

In 1936 I took up an appointment as Assistant Professor of Apologetics at the University of Notre Dame, Indiana. I returned to Notre Dame in the Fall Semesters of 1937 and 1938 and resigned when I knew that war was inevitable. When I met my class in 1936 I set them a simple examination paper to discover which of them, if any, possessed an elementary knowledge of apologetics. I asked them how they would reply to a series of stock criticisms which non-Catholics so often raise in any general discussion of religion.

The tenth question was, "How would you defend the Resurrection against a sceptic?" If I had been marking up to a maximum of one hundred only one member of my class would have been given half marks. The solitary nun in my class would have earned less than twenty-five marks. Very few of the class would have scored more than twenty-five marks, and yet my class consisted exclusively of Catholics who had been educated in Catholic schools and who had all obtained the usual credits in the apologetics classes. Indeed they joined my class because they believed themselves to have a specialist's interest in Catholic apologetics, yet, with one exception, no member of that class could have put up a creditable performance if involved in a chance argument with a non-Catholic. So far as they were concerned the teaching of apologetics had been a complete failure.

With one exception the answers to the question, "How would you defend the Resurrection?" were *lamentable*. To begin with, the answers invariably assumed much which it was their business to prove, following in this respect one textbook of apologetics widely used in Catholic schools. This particular book was the work of a priest who clearly had never suffered from any doubts himself, and who had never had to defend his beliefs against the cross-examination of a sceptic. Public debate with unbelievers is an admirable preparation for the writing of apologetics.

The main outline of the case for the Resurrection can be summarized as follows. We know that Christianity originated in the belief that Christ had risen from the dead. Unless the tomb in which he had been buried had been empty the Apostles would have preached the Resurrection in vain. The Sanhedrin, who had to account for the empty tomb, insisted that the disciples must have stolen the body. If they had stolen the body they would have known that Jesus had not risen from the dead. Why then should they face virtual certainty of death by martyrdom to propagate what they knew to be a monstrous and superfluous lie?

To this ancient controversy I made two slight contributions in my book *The Third Day.* First, I reminded the reader that the explanation put forward by the Sanhedrin, who had every interest in refuting the Resurrection, deserves far more consideration than the explanation advanced many centuries later by men whose hypothesis cannot be tested, as the hypothesis of the Sanhedrin can be tested, by cross-examination of *contemporary* witnesses. To put it more simply, *the Sanhedrin knew what they could get away with.*

My second point was in reply to the objection, "Your only authority for the explanation which you attribute to the Sanhedrin is St. Matthew; for all you know the Sanhedrin may have put forward a much more plausible explanation." To this I replied by summarizing the results of my researches in Jewish literature (pages 88 to 93 of my book), in which I proved that from the first the Jews had been forced to admit that the tomb was empty and that there is independent Jewish evidence for the fact that the

Sanhedrin explained the emptiness of the tomb by the alleged theft of the body.

To return to my apologetics class at Notre Dame. There was one member of the class who understood how the Resurrection could be defended. I was curious to discover which Catholic school had produced this prodigy, and when I congratulated him he replied, "There was an English convert on the Faculty last year, Mr. Christopher Hollis. I suppose I must have been taught about the Resurrection at school, but Mr. Hollis, *he* made it sound really interesting."

Many years ago Frank Sheed wrote a fable.

"A non-Catholic mentioned an objection to the Faith and a Catholic answered him."

It is not, of course, quite as bad as all that. The well-equipped Catholic apologist who can deal with objections to the Faith is not a fabulous monster like the griffin or the unicorn. He does exist, but he takes some finding.

I have been lecturing to Catholic schools and colleges in my own country and in America for nearly a quarter of a century, and have again and again asked my audience, or smaller groups whom I met after the lecture, how they would defend the Resurrection. I suppose I must have put the question to five thousand Catholics, products of a Catholic education. So far *not one* has given a convincing reply.

I said something to this effect in the course of a talk to an admirable Catholic girls' school in England, and added that I did not intend to put them on the spot by inviting volunteers to prove that I was wrong. The headmistress interjected a remark to the effect that she would be quite happy to accept my challenge. She called on one of the star pupils to defend the Resurrection. The result was embarrassing to the star pupil.

I have just reread the essay which Mr. Hollis contributed to a symposium which I edited, *Public School Religion*, in which he described the teaching of apologetics at Stonyhurst. It would seem from what he writes that had I put the question, "How would you defend the Resurrection?" to a group of boys at Stonyhurst, the result would have modified my experiences elsewhere, and there are, I am sure, other schools in which apologetics is as well taught as at Stonyhurst.

A Swiss priest who heard my confession and who recognized the penitent once gave me excellent advice. "You travel a great deal and hear many languages and find many different customs but there is one thing which is always the same, the Catholic Church, and wherever you go you will always have to apologise for her." He meant, of course, "to defend her", for the word "apologise" is derived from a Greek word which means "to speak on behalf of, to defend". Unfortunately many Catholics tend to be "apologetic" in the modern rather than in the original sense of the word.

It was my practice at Notre Dame to challenge my pupils to reply to popular charges against the Church. In our correspondence, published under the title *Is Christianity True?*, C. E. M. Joad was rash enough to commit himself to the statement that the "exponents of Christianity burnt the men who discovered the earth's motion, burnt the men who made the first tentative beginnings of physics and chemistry, burnt the men who laid the foundations of medical knowledge".

Every member of my class attempted to explain or excuse these wholly imaginary holocausts. Not one asked, "Whom did the Church burn and when? Names and dates, please."

By "the men who discovered the earth's motion" I suppose Joad meant the men who discovered that the earth revolved around the sun. The book in which this discovery was first published was written by Canon Copernicus and dedicated to a Pope. The expenses of publication were paid for by two Cardinals. Copernicus was greatly honoured for his discovery. "In the generation which saw the Thirty Years' War", wrote the late Professor A. N. Whitehead, F.R.S., "and remembered Alva in the Netherlands, the worst that happened to men of science was that Galileo suffered an honourable detention and a mild reproof before dying peacefully in his bed."

Bruno, who was burnt for heresy, was primarily a philosopher with an incidental interest in science. Nobody took exception to his scientific views. He was tried and condemned for theological heresy. Heresy was a capital offence then as murder is now. It would be as rational to maintain that the British persecuted dental scientists because Crippen, a dentist, was hanged for murdering his wife, as to accuse the Church of persecuting scientists because Bruno was executed on a charge which had nothing whatever to do with science. The truth is that *no* scientist was ever burnt by the Church because the Church objected to his scientific views. The persecution of scientists by the Church is part of the folk-lore of secularists. The persecution of scientists by atheists is a fact of contemporary history. It was not until a great Christian country, Russia, apostatized and adopted atheism as its state philosophy that the persecution of scientists began.[1]

It is sadly symptomatic of our age that my students should have begun by assuming that a well-known writer and university professor, such as Joad, must have got his

[1] See Chapter XVIII of my book *The Revolt Against Reason* for the evidence in support of this statement.

facts right. Catholics never allow enough for honest error; still less for the deliberate fabrication of charges against the Church. Those who had any connection with what was politely called "political warfare" find it easier to detect evidence of the carefully planned circularising of damaging rumours. Here is a case in point. Shortly before I left England for America in 1943 a friend of mine told me that some American sailors had been involved in a fight because they had gone into a pub in Portsmouth and asked for drinks "as quick as you guys got out of Dunkirk". Twenty American sailors, I was assured, were in hospital. I had hardly landed in America before an Anglophil friend of mine remarked sadly, "The British do not always make it easy for their friends in America. Twenty British sailors are in hospital as the result of a brawl. They went into a bar near the docks and demanded drinks 'as quick as you guys got out of the Philippines'." Both rumours were planted by German agents.

"Political Warfare" did not stop with the war. The Communists are indeed quite as ingenious as the Nazis in planting stories to create bad blood between Britain and the United States. When journalists ask me the same question from one end of the States to the other, it is not unreasonable to suspect a planted rumour. On my last visit to the States I was constantly asked why the Americans are detested in Europe. To which the reply was easy. Some Americans are disliked, some arouse no feelings one way or another, and the majority are liked.

Catholics seldom make sufficient allowances for the inventive talents of the Church's enemies. Our *first* reaction, then, to any particular charge against the Church should be to assume that it is unfounded. Our *second* reaction is to demand corroborative evidence and to refuse to discuss the accusation until it has been proved. Our *third* reaction must be counter-attack. If, for instance, the persecution of scientists by the Church is alleged we should contrast the excellent record of the Church, which has consistently encouraged scientific research, and the deplorable record of atheistic Russia which both under Lenin and Stalin savagely persecuted scientists whose views did not conform to Marxist orthodoxy.

Is the Church Militant a figure of speech? Is it the height of our ambition to prevent Catholics being infected with heresy, or are we making any effort in our Catholic schools and universities to produce an élite corps of Catholics competent and anxious to engage the enemies of the Faith in dialectical combat? What should we think of a boxing coach whose only ambition was to produce pupils who could be very effective in hitting a punch ball but who were under strict instructions to keep out of the ring?

A boxer can learn a lot from a good coach and can even pick up useful hints from a book on boxing, but he can only master the art of self-defence by meeting real opponents in the ring. Similarly a defender of the Faith can learn a great deal from a good teacher, or from the literature of apologetics, but no mere reading or study can take the place of the experience a man gains against real opponents in the dialectical ring.

Towards the end of my last Semester at Notre Dame I tried to supplement my lectures with practical experience of controversy. I invited a Methodist minister, an agnostic and a Communist to meet my class for tea to be followed by a friendly discussion. My boys did not do too badly at this first meeting and those who got the worst of the discussion were so nettled that they did much better next time. We did not convert the Communist but our efforts were not wholly wasted. Shortly after I left Notre Dame one of my students met the Communist in a bookshop.

"You'll be surprised", said the Communist, "to see what I've just bought", and he showed him the book *Rebuilding a Lost Faith*. "You guys", he continued, "didn't convert me to Catholicism but you put one thing across. To be a Catholic made you feel mighty good. A friend of mine, a Catholic, is losing his faith and I guess he'd be mighty unhappy without it. So I've bought this book to help him keep it." I have often wondered whether that Communist ended up in the Church. The Methodist minister who came to our party made one remark which made me think. "This is the first time", he said, "that anybody from Notre Dame has taken the slightest interest in any of us Protestants in South Bend."

Would it have been completely convincing to reply that Notre Dame was founded to provide an education for Catholics and not to convert or fraternize with South Bend Protestants? If the kind of discussion group which I began to organize towards the end of my last semester in Notre Dame were developed in all Catholic colleges, and between Newman Societies and other societies in non-Catholic universities, three results would follow. The Catholics who took part in these discussions would find in them an ideal education in apologetics; some converts would be made; and finally, many prejudices against the Church would be softened. Most of the bitterness which the Church provokes has little or no connection with Catholic dogma. Any form of ascendancy creates enemies, political, racial or religious. The ascendancy of the Catholic Church is conceded without argument by agnostics who might be described as neutrals in the controversy between Catholics and Protestants, and admitted by implication by most Protestants. And this being so, we should do all in our power to soften the inevitable effect of claims which we must support because we believe them to be true but which are inevitably irritating to those who do not accept them. The Methodist minister from South Bend obviously thought of Catholics as snooty people who disliked and despised all other Christians, and our meeting did much to disabuse him of this illusion.

Notre Dame is a spiritual power house. It is not only a university but a seminary for the Order. If South Bend, three miles from the university, were inhabited by a tribe of unconverted Red Indians, many of those dedicated priests whom I recall with affection and respect would have been set apart for missionary work in South Bend, for we recognize the obligation to provide missionaries *in partibus infidelium* but not apparently *in partibus semi-fidelium.*

The effect of these discussions on my students was all that I could have hoped. I wish I had started them in my first instead of my last semester. One of my students who went into business after leaving Notre Dame, brought twelve converts into the Church in four years. The conversion of England and America would not be the remote ideal that it is at present if every Catholic who has received a Catholic education averaged not three converts a year, as my pupil did, but one convert in his lifetime.

XIV

SPARRING PARTNERS

THE CREATOR has associated pleasure with many beneficent activities, the perpetuation of the human species for instance, and also with the defence of supernatural truth. The best work is done by those who are happy in their work, and I therefore make no apology for the fact that I have derived a great deal of fun out of my various controversies. It is only those foolish people who equate controversy with quarrelling who will be faintly shocked by this confession.

I remember with particular pleasure two debates in Pittsburgh in 1937 and 1938. Earl Browder, at that time the leading Communist in America and formerly Communist candidate for the Presidency, was to have debated with me. He informed my agent that he was very ill and would send a substitute. His substitute seemed to me a friendly soul, and my instinct told me that he had not got his heart in the job, so at the end of the debate I said, "I have a feeling that my opponent has serious doubts about Communism, and I hope the Catholics here will pray for his conversion." Which I am sure some of them did. Within two years my sparring partner was received into the Church. His name is Louis Budenz, and few defectors from Communism have rendered more valuable service to the free world.[1]

[1] These debates were described in *Come What May*, but it was not until some years after that book was published that I discovered who my opponent had been, and was reminded by somebody who had been present of

The Pittsburgh Reds felt that they had been badly let down by Browder and they insisted on a return match the following year. Arrangements were made to broadcast the debate over an extensive network. My opponent was to have been a well-known American journalist whose name was Allen, and our subject the Spanish Civil War, which was still raging.

Mr. Allen's plane was held up by a fog and I had the platform to myself, and what was intended to be a broadcast debate turned into a broadcast talk punctuated by angry yells from as unfriendly a crowd of Communists and near-Communists as I have ever seen gathered together under one roof. The Bishop, with whom I breakfasted next morning, told me that "it was the best show the radio has put up. Everything came through—the furious interruptions, your replies, the boos, the indignant back-chat from people who just could not stand you any longer and who hurled a parting insult as they left the hall. But I'm glad I wasn't there."

My chairman was a middle-aged lady with progressive views and a kind heart. She clearly expected that the platform would be rushed, and that she would be involved in the mêlée. "I'm sure we don't want any ill feeling," she said.

"On the contrary," I said, "I want the maximum of ill feeling. I want the Catholics who are living in comfort and security to have some idea what a Communist crowd looks like and sounds like. This particular bunch are very noisy, but powerless to bump me off. Try, however, to imagine what it would be like for a defenceless Catholic, a priest, for instance, to meet their opposite numbers in Madrid or Barcelona. So the more ill feeling we have the better."

---

the fact that I had suggested that the Catholics should pray for his conversion.

A priest rose and hurriedly left his seat. I wondered whether he disapproved of my appeal for ill feeling but he returned about ten minutes later. When we met after the meeting he said: "I went off to get my oils. I thought I might have to anoint you. I dare say we shall meet in heaven but we shall get there by different roads. I hope to avoid a violent death."

This was the kind of meeting I enjoy, but less useful than friendlier meetings, for I know the friendlier the debate the greater one's hope of making a real impression on those who are open to conviction. Had Mr. Allen turned up at Pittsburgh I am sure our debate would have been as friendly as was our subsequent meeting on a platform in New York.

Of all the debates which I have had, I only remember one which ended on a definitely unfriendly note, my debate with Mr. Joseph McCabe referred to below. In the course of a debate with Mr. Richard Crossman, M.P., at Zürich, the temperature certainly rose steadily for the first half of our discussion, and I was much amused by the discerning comment of a young Swiss who came up to me after the debate and said: "Two Swiss would never have allowed themselves to be so plain-spoken to each other as were you and Herr Crossman in the first half of the meeting, but if they had said the things to each other that you and Herr Crossman said, the debate would have ended in a real row. Because you are English you could lower the temperature in the second half of the debate so that you ended quite friendly."

In general Catholics tend to be too defensive in public or in private discussions. It is a mistake to give the impression of a plucky goalkeeper doing his best against a devastating attack. Every attack should be followed by a counter-attack. I remember, for instance, a debate with an atheist in London who brought up the question of the

Index. I have never met an English Catholic who had the least idea what books were actually on the Index. As a gesture of respect for ecclesiastical authority I asked the Cardinal Archbishop of Westminster for permission to read any book which I wanted to read for my own instruction, and permission was at once granted. Almost the only people who could tell you what books are on the Index are ardent freethinkers and they usually tell you wrong.

In reply to my opponent I said: "My opponent is a materialist. He does not believe in free will. He is therefore predetermined not to read the books which he hasn't read. His Index is much more restrictive than the Catholic Index, for whereas I who believe in free will am free to read and indeed have read the atheist's case against the Church, it is clear that he has never read, and on his own showing, was prevented by iron necessity from reading, any sense on the subject of religion. He calls himself a free thinker but on his own hypothesis he cannot think freely. And even if the other free thinkers present here tonight could think freely they are not encouraged to indulge in this dangerous liberty. The literature on sale outside this hall is confined to propaganda for atheism. If you people were free thinkers you would sell and buy books by Christians so that after reading both sides of the case you could freely arrive at a conclusion on the evidence instead of a conclusion imposed on you by propaganda tracts."

"Would a Catholic bookshop," I was asked, "sell propaganda for atheism?"

"They would and do," I replied.

My opponent naturally assumed that I had misunderstood the question, which was therefore repeated.

"Of course", I said, "we don't encourage simple Catholics to read the kind of tendentious propaganda your society produces, because it requires some experience to detect specious fallacies, but we think it all to the good that they should read the case for atheism within the covers of a book in which that case is met and answered. That is why the Catholic Book of the Month Club chose *Science and the Supernatural*, a correspondence between one of your champions, Professor J. B. S. Haldane, F.R.S., and myself, and why that book is on sale in Catholic bookshops such as Burns and Oates, but it is *not* on sale on your bookstall."

I have mentioned the debate with Joseph McCabe, an ex-Franciscan friar and a pillar of the Rationalist Press Association. Our subject was "Miracles". Just before leaving for the debate, which was organized by the Catholics at the University of London, I hunted in vain for my notes and as I could not find them I picked up a book which happened to be lying on a table, Alexis Carrel's *Man the Unknown*. Carrel was, as I have said in an earlier chapter, a distinguished scientist and Nobel Prize winner who went to Lourdes as a sceptic and was converted by the miracles which he witnessed. It was clear to me at an early stage of the debate that McCabe was an unscrupulous debater. He implied that one of those who had been cured at Lourdes died of venereal disease, a gross slander for which, when challenged, he could produce no evidence whatever. In point of fact the woman in question died in old age after living a life of near-sanctity. Then suddenly I heard him say, "The famous scientist and Nobel Prize winner Alexis Carrel was challenged by Father Benson to go to Lourdes. He accepted the challenge and returned to tell the world that the miracles of Lourdes were fake miracles."

I wrote down what he said and read it to my audience. "We have heard a lot tonight", I said, "about fake miracles. Now, fake miracles no more refute genuine miracles than fake quotations, such as the quotation which you have heard, refute genuine quotations such as the quotation from Carrel which I shall now read to you."

I then read a long passage in which Carrel affirms his belief that miracles entirely inexplicable as the result of suggestion have been proved to occur at Lourdes.

There was an amusing account of this debate in an article which that lively Catholic journalist, Mr. W. J. Igoe, contributed to *Duckett's Register* (March 1957).

> McCabe, God rest him, was an unlovable, wizened sort of fellow who looked as if his soul had shrunken to the size of a pea, steeped as it was in hatred. He was out to down the Church and to demonstrate that Arnold Lunn was not only deluded but something of an intellectual card-sharper. This I found very funny; Sir Arnold's method in debate is simple, almost Victorian; he lays all his cards on the table and wins because his cards are better than the other fellow's. McCabe solemnly thought him to be a "Jesuitical" rogue. Sir Arnold was a kindly if vehement Father-Confessor. . .
>
> Poor McCabe caught a courteous Tartar. Every point he raised was capped by Lunn, who could remember the books quoted and refer the quotations back to their sources. The high spot of the evening came when the poor old "rationalist" gentleman quoted a striking passage from Dr. Alexis Carrel's book on Lourdes which Lunn blandly asserted was not in the book. McCabe contradicted him. Lunn put a hand in his jacket pocket, took out a copy of the volume in question, placed it on the table and challenged his opponent. The passage was not in the book; it was not in any book. As I reported at the time, Joseph McCabe

is the only man I ever have seen floored from a sitting position. He examined the volume as if it were impregnated with deadly germs. Professor Haldane, who had been giving him rather inadequate support from the floor, beat a hasty retreat before the Catholic champion got around to demolishing *his* arguments. I asked Sir Arnold afterwards just how he had foreseen that McCabe would use the bogus quotation. "I didn't foresee anything", was the answer. "I just happened to see the book as I was leaving home and absent-mindedly stuck it in my pocket. I expect some good nun was praying for me. They do, you know."

There are moments when I am inclined to attribute my controversial luck to the fact that my debates often receive preliminary advertisement, and to the possibility that nuns remember me on these occasions in their prayers. In debating, as in games, skill is not the only important factor. Getting the breaks may be decisive in an even match. A lucky break similar to that which came my way in my debate with McCabe may be cited in support of my half-serious, half-jocular comment to Igoe.

In the autumn of 1937 I left South Bend for Chicago to debate the Spanish War with Professor, now Senator, Douglas, and at that time my opponent was a distinguished Professor at Chicago University. I did not bother to make any notes, for I was at home in that particular controversy, but I bought a book at the railway bookstall to pass the time in the train. The book opened with some interesting letters from the Spanish Front by members of the International Brigade, and ended with an article by Mr. Allen, with whom I was to have debated in Pittsburgh, on the alleged massacre of the Reds after the capture of Badajoz. This story was first published in the *New York Herald Tribune* on the authority of a reputable American journalist, Mr. Reynolds Packard. Mr. Packard, however, who was in Portugal at the time of the alleged massacre and whose signature to the telegram had been written in by a Red, vigorously protested against the misuse of his name.

I was impressed by Professor Douglas' sincerity, and I knew of him as a distinguished scholar with a scholar's respect for sources. I realized at once that he must have been misled by some unreliable source when, in all good faith, he cited Mr. Allen as an eye-witness of the massacre.

"He never witnessed the massacre and never claimed to have witnessed it," I interjected, "he was merely reporting what Reds told him. Here is what he actually wrote." And I handed him the book. Professor Douglas at once admitted that he had been mistaken, but if I had not providentially bought that book with no other purpose in view but entertainment, the effect of my rejoinder would have been far less convincing. That is what I mean by luck in debating.

I remember that debate for another reason. As we left the hall Professor Douglas said, "It's pleasant to discover that I can entertain a really friendly feeling for my opponent after a debate such as this on which you and I differ so profoundly." I have always regretted that we have not met since.

A Catholic debater is to some extent handicapped by past history. Whatever an educated non-Catholic may believe, the underworld of the opposition associates us with Torquemada and assumes that we instinctively detest and despise all those whom we classify as heretics. And if debates achieve no other purpose than to correct this illusion they will be worth while.

One must begin by assuming that one's opponents are

in good faith until the contrary is proved. Nothing makes a better impression on an audience than a candid admission that difficulties are difficulties. I remember how dissuasive I found, and still find, all attempts to suggest that the reconciliation of omniscience and free will is not a real difficulty. Moreover, it never does any harm and often does a great deal of good to concede a point and to compliment one's opponent on an able statement of his case.

When I first met the sparring partner who debated with me first before the university and then in the city of Melbourne, he was obviously carrying an outsize chip on his shoulder. When he discovered that I did not dislike him at sight and was grateful for his co-operation he began to melt. His supporters at the debate in the town began by being very hostile, but after I had coaxed a few laughs out of them they too softened, and at the end of the debate they gave me a really generous clap. "Is the Church inherently intolerant?" was the theme of our debate, and I suppose my opponent must have felt that I was not exactly an advertisement for this inherent intolerance of the Church, because he took the trouble to warn the audience that I was not, in his opinion, a typical Catholic.

"Some men", he remarked, "are better than their creeds." Reeling under the absurdity of this suggestion that I was a better man than the average Catholic, I could only reply that no man was good enough to live up to the Catholic code or bad enough to live down to atheism.

The most useful form of debating is the debate in book form because the book remains long after the memory of a verbal debate is forgotten.

I have engaged in four such debates; with Ronald Knox before I became a Catholic (*Difficulties*), with Cyril Joad (*Is Christianity True?*) and with Professor J. B. S. Haldane,

F.R.S. (*Science and the Supernatural*) and Dr. G. G. Coulton (*Is the Catholic Church Anti-Social?*). Of my debate with Ronald Knox I have written in this book, of my debate with C. E. M. Joad in my book *Memory to Memory*. Joad appeared to have read no philosopher between Aristotle and Bernard Shaw, and his contributions to our joint book were therefore valuable as an anthology of popular errors about the Catholic Church in general and medievalism in particular.

J. B. S. Haldane was a more formidable but less friendly sparring partner. Our first real meeting was at Mürren in the 'twenties. My father, who at that time was chairman of the Palace Hotel, enjoyed inviting eminent Englishmen to lecture to his guests, and *therefore* persuaded himself that the said eminences would attract many visitors to the hotel, which in point of fact they did not.

When we met at Mürren, Haldane was still Reader in Biochemistry at Cambridge and a member of the Senior Common Room at Trinity. He had just married a lady whose marriage to her previous husband had been terminated. Haldane retained his Readership in spite of an academic storm provoked by the circumstances of his marriage, and he was, I suspect, agreeably surprised that my father had been wholly uninfluenced by this Cambridge fuss.

My wife and I liked the Haldanes and often had tea with them on a terrace outside the hotel. My wife was impressed by Charlotte Haldane's uncanny knack of picking out four-leaved clover. Mrs. Haldane was a Jewess and from time to time Haldane would interject a defiant remark, "My wife being a Jewess." It was with some difficulty that I suppressed a temptation to counter with "My wife being a Christian."

Haldane was well-born, and the nephew of Lord Haldane. He had been educated at Eton and New College,

Oxford. He had indeed the ideal background for a left-winger, for he could make depreciatory remarks about the aristocracy and public schools without being suspected of envy. He enjoyed the best of both worlds, for it was as fashionable in intellectual circles to be left-wing as it was to be Etonian in social circles. He achieved at a comparatively early age that most coveted of scientific distinctions, the right to add F.R.S. after his name. He had fought with distinction in the First World War and had proved himself embarrassingly courageous—embarrassingly, for his fellow-officers, who accepted the normal risks philosophically, were often irritated by Haldane's puckish delight in positively attracting enemy fire. After the war he made a series of dangerous experiments on his own body in the interests of biological research. He was and is a very brave man.

The Haldanes did nothing to ingratiate themselves with Cambridge society. In spite of his outstanding qualifications he was not elected a Fellow of Trinity. "I rank with the Chaplain at Trinity," he remarked with disgust, "we're neither of us Fellows." In due course he left Cambridge and accepted the Professorship of Biochemistry at University College, London.

Later he became associated with the Communist Party as chairman of the editorial board of the *Daily Worker* though he was, I believe, never a member of the Communist Party. I have often wondered whether in his case, as in so many others, his association with Communism was not, in part at least, the consequence of frustrated ambition. His relationships with the *Daily Worker* were never happy, and he finally broke with the Communists as the result of the persecution of scientists in Soviet Russia.

Our controversy was not particularly friendly. Haldane flattered himself that he was one of those exceptional secularists who have taken the trouble to read St. Thomas Aquinas. My criticisms of his scientific beliefs did not ruffle him, but he lost his temper when I convicted him of attributing to St. Thomas a belief which in point of fact St. Thomas got into trouble for repudiating. He was angry when I mildly suggested that it is not easy to understand St. Thomas unless one knows something about the intellectual background of his age.

Catholics are much better informed on the case against Catholicism than atheists on the case against atheism, as was only too apparent in this controversy. Haldane assumed, of course, that the result would be a walk-over. I have never heard of anybody being converted to atheism by Haldane's arguments, but I know of two converts to the Church who were influenced by this book. Miss Phyllis Holt-Needham, who was at that time my secretary, was one of them. When she came to me she had lost her faith, and was under the influence of the moderns. Of course she confidently expected that Haldane would make rings round me and was both irritated and annoyed by his failure. At first she was inclined to attribute his lack of success to my controversial talents, but before the last letter had been written she was beginning to suspect that it was the strength of my case which enabled me to put up such a surprisingly good show against a man who was my intellectual superior, and it was to Haldane rather than to Arnold Lunn that Phyllis really owes her conversion to the Catholic Church. My book with Haldane had also some influence, so he tells me, on Lord Pakenham's conversion. "Arnold Lunn's controversy with Haldane", he writes in *Born to Believe*, "removed my sneaking suspicion that in a real showdown there would be materialistic questions the man of religion could not face."

Haldane and I have at least one thing in common. We are both fantastically absent-minded. It was therefore not surprising that Haldane, who had volunteered to collect the typescript of my chapters from my office and then take them with his own contribution to the publisher, should have left one of my chapters in the taxicab. I rang him up when the loss was discovered. "Unfortunately I cannot, like an evolutionist, appeal to the missing links in my argument, so please find the missing chapter." Luckily I had a copy.

My last controversy was with that pugnacious old gentleman the late Dr. G. G. Coulton. I am inclined to think that Coulton might conceivably have found his way into the Church had he been more wisely handled in his controversy with Cardinal Gasquet. Coulton discovered many errors in one of the Cardinal's books, and received a rather frosty acknowledgement of his services in this respect. Doubtless Coulton's letter had not been a model of tact. The Cardinal subsequently reprinted the book with all the errors uncorrected.

Dr. Coulton attached great importance to academic distinction himself, and his name as author of the most insignificant of pamphlets was always followed by a string of letters, Litt.D., D.Litt., etc. He was certainly in no danger of underestimating the importance of a Prince of the Church. If, then, the Cardinal had replied politely to his letter, thanked him courteously for drawing his attention to obvious mistakes, promised to correct these in a new edition, and asked the good doctor to lunch at the Athenaeum, he would have made a friend of Coulton for life.

When we find, as in the case of Dr. Coulton, a venomous hatred for the Church which is unusual among civilized people who can appreciate the cultural debt which the world owes to the Church of Dante, Michelangelo and the architects of St. Mark's, Salisbury Cathedral and Chartres, it is always wise to suspect some personal slight.

Is there, perhaps, some such explanation of the pathological dislike which the Church evokes in that brilliant writer, Professor Hugh Trevor-Roper? One need not be a Catholic to find his tone distressing. That urbane humanist, Sir Harold Nicolson, reviewing his *Historical Essays* in *The Observer* (20 October 1957), writes:

> . . . There were moments when the pleasure that this book has given me was riven by a painful suspicion that the Professor was harsh . . . among the strings of his lute there is a wire of hate which is apt to twang suddenly with the rasp of a banjo. Why need he refer to Scotland, a haven of romance and sober learning, as "that prosaic peninsula"? Why should he allow his Protestant bias to cloud the compassion that he ought to feel for the Jesuit martyrs, to sneer at Farm Street, or to contend that "at no time have the English Catholics been an active or progressive element in the nation"? How can a writer of his distinction permit himself the atrocious phrase: "Even in England, converts to Popery are generally regarded as socially *déclassés*"? One might forgive such passages were they due solely to a lack of taste; Mr. A. J. P. Taylor has also been guilty of some ugly sayings; but with him we feel they derive from a sense of mischief, whereas with Professor Trevor-Roper we feel that there is an absence of even average human compassion. I may be sentimental, but I mind such gaps in sympathy very much indeed . . .

Dr. Coulton made a practice of issuing challenges to leading Catholics to debate with him, in book form, papal infallibility or the social record of the Church. From time to time he published the names of those who had declined his challenges. Catholics who understood

Coulton's limitations greatly underestimated the propaganda effect of Coulton's reiterated boast that no Catholic dared to meet him in debate.

I, for one, was persuaded that Coulton was fully justified in a claim which it fell to me in later years to prove untenable, the claim advanced in the following passage. "There is no Roman Catholic writer with a real sense of responsibility (let us say a recognised university teacher or a prominent Jesuit, or a man whom the bishop of his diocese would vouch for as a competent champion of his Church) who would dare to discuss by fair reply and counter-reply the historical question of papal infallibility, or the crooked methods of Roman Catholic historians in the past and up to the present day."[1]

Every individual Catholic whom Coulton challenged was fully entitled to decline to turn away from work which interested him to debate with Coulton. Of all the published debates in which I have been engaged my debate with Coulton was the most tedious, because he had not the remotest idea of sticking to any point long enough to discuss it thoroughly. His second letter was not less than eighty-five pages in length. But though every individual could be forgiven for his reluctance to face the tedium of a Coulton controversy, the effect of every challenge being declined was deplorable. If there had been in existence the kind of society which I believe would be invaluable, an official society of Catholic debaters, Coulton's challenges would have been addressed to this society, which would have provided a Catholic both willing and competent to accept his challenge.

Shortly after I became a Catholic I informed the good doctor that I would be enchanted to take him on. He

[1] Quoted by me in *Is the Catholic Church Anti-Social?* My subsequent references are to this book.

replied with a contemptuous negative. I provoked him into a correspondence in which he underlined the contrast between his academic standing and my lack of qualifications. As he had announced his intention of publishing our correspondence I extracted puckish delight from prolonging it in order to wind up my last letter with a sentence to the effect that the good doctor had spent fifty pounds publishing a correspondence in order to demonstrate beyond all possibility of doubt that I was too unimportant to correspond with G. G. Coulton, D.Lit., Litt.D., etc.

In 1943 Dr. Coulton broadcast yet another challenge and Dr. John Heenan, now Archbishop of Liverpool, in a letter to the *Catholic Herald* of 10 November 1943, suggested that I should accept it. By this time I had satisfied the various conditions which he laid down in the passage mentioned, for I had taught at Notre Dame and was authorized to debate with Dr. Coulton by the Cardinal Archbishop of Westminster. Dr. Coulton's Protestant supporters do not seem to have shared his confidence in victory for all his attempts to find a publisher failed. Fortunately Holy Church came to the rescue of the enemy of Holy Church.

Burns and Oates, publishers to the Holy See, were quite willing to publish the book provided that the Cardinal had no objection. The Cardinal was delighted. Not so the censor. I submitted to the censor each letter as written in order to deprive Dr. Coulton of any excuse for suggesting that my interpretation of Catholic doctrine, where we differed, was correct and not a private interpretation which the Church would disown. The censor, as I learned through another priest, was horrified at the idea of the Church giving any sort of *Imprimatur* to a book which contained so many lurid insults to the Church in general and to many Popes in particular. It would not, of course, have been practicable to lead off with *Omnia obstant*, pp. 1–18; *Nihil obstat*, pp. 19–40; *Omnia obstant*, pp. 41–120.

Once again I appealed to the Cardinal. He sent for my letter and asked me round in the evening. "I've just got your letter", he said. "To prevent further waste of time I'm going to censor it myself. Meanwhile there's a bottle of whisky. Help yourself." An odd situation. Few laymen can have had the privilege of drinking some excellent whisky while a Prince of the Church censored something that they had written. When he had finished reading my letter, which he passed without comment, he said, "You'd better choose your own censor, somebody who will not merely give you an *imprimatur* for each letter but somebody you can consult on some knotty point." So I suggested the Jesuits at Heythrop, who specialize in current controversy, and very helpful they were.

Dr. Coulton was by far the least formidable of my four debating opponents. He had admittedly collected a vast store of facts about the Middle Ages, but he was not an outstanding expert in the period. He relied far too much on unreliable secondary sources such as the American H. C. Lea, author of various works on the Inquisition, Indulgences, etc. When Father Herbert Thurston, S.J., casually remarked in a review that "in any ten consecutive pages [of any of Lea's books] ten palpable blunders may be unearthed", Coulton promptly sent him twelve pages selected from one of Lea's books, and in his own words invited Father Thurston to transform himself into "the providentially ordained instrument for exploding Lea (and incidentally me) once for all". Father Thurston discovered fifteen palpable blunders in the twelve pages selected, not one of which Coulton tried to defend. The double explosion was complete. The truth is, of course, that Father Thurston was, and Dr. Coulton was not, an outstanding authority on the Middle Ages.

I recently reviewed a history of mountaineering by an Alpine equivalent of H. C. Lea, and detected about one mistake in every page. Had I written of this author in the eulogistic terms in which Coulton invariably wrote of Lea I should renounce all hope of being accepted as an authority on Alpine history.

In our own correspondence Dr. Coulton was at least as impenitent in error as Cardinal Gasquet. On pp. 198–206 I summarized a succession of glaring errors, including mistranslations from medieval Latin. He had made virtually no attempt to defend any of these errors. I do not for one moment deny that Dr. Coulton had acquired a mass of information about the Middle Ages, but he remained to the end astonishingly ignorant of elementary facts about the Catholic Church. He assumed, to take one instance, that an Irish Catholic was bound to confess to his own parish priest, an elementary howler of which no Catholic however ill-instructed would be capable.

The Protestant press virtually ignored the book, the only important Protestant paper to review it being *The Irish Times*. I have mislaid the review but the general tone was one of sorrow that Dr. Coulton, who was obviously in the right, had not been able to convict his slippery opponent of error.

In spite of all the vituperation of which the Church and I were the target I never succeeded in disliking Dr. Coulton. There was something really lovable about the old warrior. If the anti-Catholic bee had not buzzed so loudly and so continuously in his bonnet he would have enriched our literature with works which Catholics would have enjoyed and admired. His prose at its best was superb, and there were many aspects of the Church with which he was in obvious sympathy. He certainly deserved the tribute of a great Benedictine scholar, Dom Moray, who wrote: "Dr. Coulton's pamphlets and controversies are already partly forgotten and will be completely buried by time; I prefer to think that his name will live as the author of the most beautiful chapter on St. Bernard in our time."

XV

"A UNITED CHRISTIAN FRONT"

IN THE last decade before the Second World War it was routine for Protestants to record their sympathy with Pastor Niemöller, whom Hitler had imprisoned, and with the Jewish victims of Nazi persecution. At the Methodist Conference of 1938 my father, the late Sir Henry Lunn, moved an amendment to include in this vote of sympathy the persecuted Catholics in Spain. The amendment was carried, and the Methodists have the unique distinction of being the only Protestants officially to go on record as protesting against a persecution of Christians more severe than any since the time of Diocletian. In America four hundred Protestant ministers signed a manifesto, published in the American Press, in which they proclaimed their support of a Government in whose territory almost every church was destroyed, defiled or closed, and in which the few surviving priests who had not been murdered, were in hiding.

My father appealed in *The Times* for a united Christian front against the forces of militant atheism, and to this appeal Cardinal Hinsley, Archbishop of Westminster, replied,

> Those who belong to the Catholic and Roman Church will have read with appreciation and respect Sir Henry Lunn's moving appeal in your columns for a united Christian Front against the world-wide anti-

Christian onslaught. Pius XI explicitly appeals in his letter *Divini Redemptoris* to all who believe in God. Between those who believe in Christ as true God and true Man and worship him, there should be charity—an effort to draw nearer to him and so nearer to one another. This means not only friendly relationship but mutual help in defending the civilization which is founded on the truths enunciated in the Nicene Creed. Sir Henry rightly insists on this bond between us. Let us be frank. There have been in the past misunderstandings and faults of manner on both sides, and of temper and lack of charity in controversy. These, our failings and differences, the enemies of religion have exploited. But the realization of a common peril is drawing Christians together in practical sympathy.

Cardinal Hinsley, whose memory I revere and for whose intercession I hope, was genuinely anxious to promote that friendly co-operation between all Christians of good will which has been warmly recommended more than once by the present Pope, and it was indeed in the hope of creating a united Christian front that the *Sword of the Spirit* was founded in July 1940, its primary objective being the co-operation of Christians in resistance against tyranny and in all that concerns the temporal welfare of mankind.

At the Sword of the Spirit meetings Catholics, Anglicans and Dissenters spoke from the same platform, and for a time it seemed as if the relations between Catholics and Protestants were definitely improving. These activities, however, did not meet with universal approval among Catholics. Many influential Catholics feared lest the appearance on the same platform of Catholics and Protestants might encourage among marginal Catholics tendencies to "indifferentism", that is, to the error that it is a matter of indifference to which Christian Communion one belongs. Catholics who were actively associated with such meetings had no such fears. On the contrary, they had learned from experience that many a non-Catholic at these meetings had been impressed by the contrast between the clarity and confidence with which Catholic speakers applied unchanging principles to the solution of temporal problems and the hesitancy which from time to time found expression in the speeches of the occasional Protestants who had been influenced by modernism.

Admittedly, if these joint meetings had encouraged among the less stable Catholics the illusion that the different Churches were like different clubs, and that the wise man selected the Church or club to suit his tastes and his temperament, some Catholics might have been tempted to resign from the Catholic Church and seek membership in a Christian Church far less exacting than the Catholic in its attitude to marriage. I do not myself believe that there is any solid basis for such anxiety. The overwhelming majority of those who leave the Church because they rebel against the Church's teaching on marriage and contraception do not join other Christian Communions, but exchange a supernatural for a secularist philosophy. An occasional Catholic becomes an Anglican or Nonconformist but the quality of such converts is unremarkable.

So far from fearing lest a "United Christian Front" would lead to secessions from the Church, my own conviction is that it would, if anything, increase the number of converts, for one of the major dissuasions which prevent so many potential converts from examining the case for the Church is the conviction that the attitude of Catholics to other Christians is intolerant and uncharitable, but the removal of this obstacle to conversion is not the main reason for desiring friendlier relations between Catholics and Protestants. Cordial co-operation is desirable because neither Catholics nor Protestants have anything to gain from unfriendly relations, the only beneficiary of such animosities being the common enemy of all Christians, Soviet Russia.

The Sword of the Spirit still exists, but it did not long continue to organize joint meetings at which both Catholics and Protestants spoke. The Anglicans at the outset not unnaturally expected that they would be represented on the *Sword* Committee and tended to lose interest when it became clear that membership of the *Sword* was exclusively Catholic. The cause of co-operation also suffered from the fact that on the crucial issue of religious education the Anglicans, who were far less interested in maintaining their schools than were the Catholics, were half-hearted in their attitude to the new Education Act. Moreover many Catholics complain that co-operative committees, such as those on which Christians and Jews serve, are very active when Jews or Protestants are being persecuted but less interested when Catholics are the victims of persecution.

It would however be foolish to underestimate the difficulties of effective co-operation between Catholics and Protestants. Indeed, the main difficulty is inherent in the very nature of the Catholic claim. From her foundation the Church has always known herself to be the trustee for supernatural truths, truths of infinite importance to mankind, and has always acted with unshaken conviction on the assumption that these truths, if not protected from corruption by the divine authority which the Church derives from her founder, Christ, would soon become infected by falsehood. The modern Catholic could cite in support of this view the fact that Christian

Communions which repudiate the authority of the Church often show a tendency to evolve into a kind of camouflaged Unitarianism. Nobody can read the New Testament with care without realizing that those aspects of Catholicism which non-Catholics regard with such distrust, Catholic exclusiveness and Catholic intolerance of heresy, are implicit in the teaching of Christ, of St. Paul and of the primitive Church.

Christ warned us that "he that believeth not shall be damned" (Mark xvi. 16[1]). Christ insisted that those who rejected the teaching of the Apostles rejected his teaching. "He that despiseth you despiseth me" (Luke x. 16).

The faith which St. Paul recommends has sharp edges and clear outlines. It demands loyalty. The brethren are exhorted to "stand fast and hold the traditions which ye have been taught, whether by word, or our epistle" (2 Thess. ii. 15). They are warned against "diverse strange doctrines". The duty of the bishop is clearly defined: "Holding fast the faithful word as he hath been taught, that he may be able by sound doctrine both to exhort and to convince the gainsayers" (Titus i. 9). The Greek word translated "gainsayers" should more properly be translated "heretics". It is, writes St. Paul, the duty of the bishops to stop the mouth of heretics who subvert "whole houses". The brethren are to avoid such heretics (Rom. xvi. 17) and "have no company" with those who are disobedient (2 Thess. ii. 6 *et seq.*).

The obstinate heretic is to be expelled. "A man that is a heretic after the first and second admonition reject" (Titus iii. 10). Finally, the heretic who "bringeth not this doctrine" is neither to be received nor sent on his journey with friendship. "Neither bid him God speed:

[1] In order not to arouse a suspicion of quoting a translation adapted to Catholic views, I am quoting from the Authorized Version.

For he that biddeth him God speed is partaker of his evil deeds" (2 John, 11).

Could anything be more explicit? If Catholic intolerance of heresy is unchristian, we must repudiate not only the Pope but St. Paul, not only St. Paul but Christ. Intolerance of heresy must not of course be confused with intolerance of heretics, though too often the former, which is right, has led to the latter, which is wrong. Had St. Augustine's rule, *diligite homines, interficite errores*, "Love man, slay errors", been consistently observed there would have been no Spanish Inquisition.

Unfortunately it is difficult to steer an even course between the Scylla of appearing discourteous to Christians of other Communions and the Charybdis of conceding by implication the possibility of compromise on points of principle. Consider, for instance, the conferences of Christians which meet from time to time to consider reunion. The first of such conferences in modern times was the Grindelwald conference summoned by my father in 1892 to consider the Reunion of the Churches.

The basic premise of all reunion conferences is that the unity of the Church has been shattered, and that the Reunion of the Churches is only possible if the different Christian Communions are prepared to compromise. Some reunionists would add that diversity of belief is not in itself a bad thing. The National Church, according to this theory, is positively enriched by the spiritual witness and experience of different schools of Anglicanism.

The basic premise of the Catholic Church is that there is only one Church which has never been divided, that the schismatic communions have left the Church which Christ founded, that there can be no question of reunion of that which has never been disunited but only of the return of the schismatics to the Church which Christ founded.

It is clear that if the Catholic Church sent official delegates to a reunion conference they would, in effect, be admitting by implication the Protestant premise that the question to be debated is not the conditions under which schismatics could return to an undivided Church but the conditions for the reunion of many Churches none of which has a monopoly of divine truth.

Now, it is unreasonable to expect the Catholics to compliment away their own case in the interests of courtesy, and it is the fear of being manœuvred into a position in which the Catholic appears to concede some part of the Protestant case which makes many Catholics reluctant to be associated with these conferences. None the less, Catholics have sometimes been permitted to be present as "observers", a gesture which commits us to nothing but which is one of those courtesies which do so much to soften existing asperities.

In their attitude to co-operation with Protestants Catholics differ as they differ on everything excepting defined doctrine. There are extreme isolationists whose ideal is the complete isolation of Catholics from Protestant contacts, and there are extreme collaborators who are sometimes in danger of forgetting the importance of insisting on the unique character of the Church. I have sometimes wondered whether the difference between the isolationist and the co-operator corresponded roughly to Ronald Knox's conception of the different roles of shepherd and fisherman, the shepherd who is mainly preoccupied with the salvation of his flock and the fisherman who hopes for a rich catch of converts.

The typical "isolationist" has lost all hope of converting the world and feels that it is a full-time job to prevent Catholics being infected by the anti-Catholic atmosphere in which they live. Consciously or unconsciously he tries to create a kind of Catholic ghetto—the phrase, by the way, was invented by a Catholic priest—in which the faithful can be protected from unnecessary contacts with heretics. The "co-operator", on the other hand, is more hopeful of influencing the world in which he lives. Far from seeking to reduce, he is anxious to multiply, contacts between Catholics and non-Catholics. For he is not so defeatist as to assume that the only result of such contacts will be to make Catholics less Catholic. On the contrary, he believes in the possibility of creating a Catholic élite who will change rather than be changed by the world.

During the twenty-five years since I became a Catholic the shift of emphasis in Catholic apologetics which dates from the nineteen-twenties has become more and more noticeable. The Protestant is increasingly regarded less as an enemy than as a co-belligerent against the forces of materialism. Catholic apologetics, as developed for instance in the pamphlets issued by the Catholic Truth Society, tends to dwell more and more on the positive arguments for the Faith and less and less on the negative criticism of other Christians. Symptomatic is the revolution in the outlook of *The Tablet*, which was edited, at the time I became a Catholic, by Ernest Oldmeadow, a convert from Methodism. As a Methodist he resented, we may be sure, the Anglican claims, and in particular the refusal of High Churchmen to recognize the Methodist ministry or the Methodist claim to belong to the Universal Church. When I was a boy, Anglicans gave great offence by refusing to use the word "Church" in connection with Nonconformists. They would write, instead, of "Nonconformist *bodies*". Oldmeadow, who had perhaps suffered from a defence complex *vis-à-vis* the Anglicans, was all the happier to feel, as a Catholic convert, that the roles had been reversed and that he could revenge himself on the Anglicans by referring, for instance, to Anglo-Catholic priests as "High Anglican ministers". He did not, however, refuse to describe Anglican bishops as bishops, which was illogical, for whereas the word "bishop" originated in the Church, the word "priest" is far older than Christianity and cannot therefore be restricted to Christians or to priests recognized by the Catholics as possessing valid orders. It is therefore not only discourteous but illogical to deny that Anglicans are priests unless one is prepared to talk about "Tibetan ministers" or the "clergymen of ancient Rome", or to rewrite the opening lines of Macaulay's "The Priest of Nemi",

> The parson that slew the slayer
> And shall himself be slain.

Ernest Oldmeadow was a devout and loyal Catholic, an agreeable companion and an excellent judge of wine, but *The Tablet* under his editorship was not a credit to the Church. The editorial notes were mainly devoted to cracks against "High Anglicans", varied by jibes against Nonconformists.

The Tablet changed hands in 1936, when Cardinal Hinsley succeeded Cardinal Bourne, and it would be difficult today to name any Catholic paper which has a greater prestige or is more widely read by non-Catholics. In its comments on non-Catholics *The Tablet* has established a tradition of doctrinal firmness combined with charity and courtesy towards those who are not of our faith, and this tradition is in the main representative of the Church in England. It would be pleasant to record a corresponding change in the attitude of the Church of

England, but Catholics far better informed on this point than I am, fear that the Anglican attitude has hardened in recent years.

Irrespective, however, of results so far achieved, we are clearly bound to work for that co-operation with Christians in other Communions for those ends approved by the present Pope, whose permission for Catholics to join with Protestants in the Our Father removes at least one source of invincible prejudice. Very welcome is the increasing tendency to take these prejudices into account in the hope of diminishing them. A case in point from my own experience may be cited.

In 1944 an Anglo-Catholic priest who had read with pleasure a book of mine, invited me to preach in his church in Hampstead. He was good enough to express his appreciation of the fact that I had never written offensively about the Church of England. The letter was so charming that I could not bring myself to refuse *sans phrase*, so I accepted his invitation subject to the consent of the Cardinal, a consent which I was convinced would *not* be given. To my great surprise Cardinal Griffin said, "I don't see why you should not accept this invitation, provided that you do not take part in the actual service." I therefore waited in the Vicar's study until it was time for me to occupy the pulpit, where I delivered what was less a sermon than a talk about the Communist threat to Christianity.

I stayed for supper, and still recall with delight a wonderful evening with good talk and a warmth of friendliness inspired by the feeling that the beliefs on which my hosts and I differed were less important than those on which we agreed. Naturally we must all be free to define the points on which we differ and to defend our own interpretations of Christianity, but *in omnibus caritas*.

It is difficult to persuade the world that the Catholic attitude to the heretic need not be intolerant. Indeed the very word "heretic" is so closely associated in the Protestant mind with fanatical intolerance in general and the stake in particular that there is an increasing reluctance among charitable Catholics to use the word. In *Memory to Memory* I quoted a letter of Cardinal Manning's to my father ("I embrace you in the soul of the Church, and rejoice in all your good works"), and a remark about my father by Cardinal Hinsley, "I should never use the word 'heretic' in talking about a man like your father who loves our Lord and who loves truth and who has always been so ready to make great sacrifices for truth." *The Methodist Times* quoted this saying of the Cardinal's with obvious pleasure.

During my own long pilgrimage to the Church the Catholics whom I found most persuasive were those who were well informed about Protestantism, and who were most generous in their appreciation of Protestant piety. Unfortunately there were occasional converts whose ungenerous attitude to the Church of their baptism neutralized their propaganda for the Church. Robert Hugh Benson was a case in point. No Anglican parson in his novels could command real respect in the readers, and this in spite of the fact that Benson, the son of an Archbishop of Canterbury and a former member of the Mirfield community, had known Anglicanism at its best. A similar criticism could be made of a satire which Knox published shortly after his conversion. Ronald Knox was never an enthusiastic co-operator, always "more of a crook than a hook" (see page 13), but in his later years he did not neglect the occasional opportunity for friendly contacts with Anglicans. The Dean of Windsor recalled in *The Times* old memories of Knox and of Oxford, and it was clear how greatly he had been touched by a letter in which Ronald Knox, shortly before his death, suggested that they should pray for each other: *oremus invicem.*

Catholics and Protestants have much to forgive and to forget. There have been in the past, as Cardinal Hinsley remarked, "faults of manners on both sides", but the growing realisation of a common threat to everything which Christians hold dear is, I hope and believe, narrowing the gulf between us. It is perhaps a happy omen of rapprochements to come that the Catholic Archbishop Heenan of Liverpool and the Anglican Archbishop of York should have spoken from a common platform and opened proceedings by an exchange of courtesies and good-humoured wit.

Since this chapter was first written I have revisited Spain, and it is, I think, worth while to add something on the treatment of Protestants there.

Nearly twenty-five years have passed since I first met Father Manuel Aleman, who was responsible for the translation into Spanish of *Now I See*. We first met in the 'twenties just after he had been turned out of the Navy because he had refused to take the oath of loyalty to the Republican régime. Father Aleman has always been an ardent monarchist and even in those days he had an interest in Catholic apologetics which is unusual in all laymen and particularly unusual in a Spanish layman. Indeed, I was startled to discover, when he lunched with me in London, that he had read *Now I See*. A few years ago his wife became a Carmelite nun and he entered the seminary in Avila, and has subsequently been ordained a secular priest.

In the course of my visit, we discussed the position of Protestants in Spain and Father Manuel offered to introduce me to the new Foreign Minister. Unfortunately my remaining day was fully occupied, so instead I put my views into a letter which he promised to bring to the attention of the Foreign Minister.

I quoted to Father Manuel a remark made to me by one of our own Catholic bishops: "If I believed that it was right for the Catholics, when they are in the majority, to give Protestants different treatment from the kind we Catholics expect when we are in a minority, I should not speak on Catholic platforms in support of our demand for generous treatment of our Catholic schools. It is dishonourable for Catholics to have two standards, according to whether they are or are not in the majority."

And in point of fact most Catholic countries act on this principle. In Quebec, Protestant schools are fully maintained by the State. In Protestant Ontario, Catholic schools receive no help. The same situation is true of Catholic cantons in Switzerland, which are generous to Protestant schools, in contrast to Protestant cantons which do nothing for Catholic schools. In Catholic Ireland the Government treats Catholic and Protestant schools on the same basis.

I made it quite clear that I had raised this question not only because I regarded it as *inexpedient* for the Spanish Hierarchy to molest Spanish Protestants—inexpedient because they thereby provide Protestants in countries where Catholics are in a minority with an excuse for making themselves disagreeable to the Catholic minority—but also because I believed such behaviour to be inconsistent with the authentic Catholic principles—though not of course with Catholic practice in the Spanish Inquisition.

I remember arguing this point with a Spanish ecclesiastic who insisted that error has no rights against truth—an odd remark for a trained theologian to make, for he must have known that neither truth nor error has rights, since rights can only be predicated of men and not of abstractions. Men in error have very definite rights, civic rights among them, and Catholics equally have a definite obligation to respect the consciences of men in error.

I know, of course, that the Spanish Hierarchy's attitude to Spanish Protestants is influenced by the fact that the overwhelming majority of Protestants throughout the world sympathized with the Red Government. During a recent visit to America there was a violent radio attack on Catholicism as the enemy of freedom. Many of the examples chosen to support this thesis were taken from Spain, beginning with the Inquisition and ending with the modern treatment of Protestants. The Press published a reply in which I stated that though I strongly disapproved of molesting Protestants I did not think that American Protestants were in a strong position to protest in view of their deplorable attitude in the Civil War.

None the less, it must not be forgotten that many prominent Protestants, my own father among them, took a splendid stand on the side of Catholic Spain.

I appreciate the fact that a Government has the right to forbid any public demonstration which is likely to create a breach of the peace. Mr. Asquith, when Home Secretary, forbade a Catholic procession to carry the Host through London streets at the time of the Eucharistic Congress, and he was fully justified in this veto in view of the threats of militant Orangemen to break up the procession. The Spaniards would be no less entitled to forbid any public demonstration of militant Protestantism which could only lead to trouble in a country as deeply Catholic as Spain and as untutored in the practice of tolerance.

Moreover, it would not be unreasonable to forbid the entry of American Protestant missionaries. Spanish Protestants, I hold, should be permitted to propagate their views by word of mouth or in book or pamphlet form, just as Danish Catholics, who are in a small minority, are free to do what they can to convert their Protestant neighbours, but the Danish Catholics would be the first to protest if foreign Catholic missionaries settled in Denmark and opened a violent campaign of insult and invective directed against the Danish Protestants. Yet this is precisely the procedure of many American Protestant missionaries in Spanish South America. I have seen some of the tracts distributed by the kind of Protestant missionary who is as devoid of culture as of charity.

I remember a conversation in Madrid in 1941 with a beautiful woman, daughter of a famous Carlist leader. She exclaimed contemptuously, "You English Catholics will never understand our Catholicism. We Spanish Catholics never compromise with the truth. *Nous ne transigeons jamais avec la vérité.*"

"If that be so," I said, "how is it that one cannot buy in Madrid the papal encyclicals against Fascism and Nazism, and that your Press never mentioned the Pope's denunciation of Nazi behaviour in Poland? I'm only an English Catholic, and what's worse a convert, but I had always understood that when the Vicar of Christ spoke it was the duty of all Catholics to listen and of all Catholic governments to give every facility for the publication of such pronouncements."

The Carlist looked embarrassed. "Well, you know, we have the Germans on the frontier."

"I know that full well," I replied, "and I am not being censorious about the censorship of Papal pronouncements, but you will understand why I am not impressed by your brave boast 'Nous ne transigeons jamais avec la vérité'. After the war you must come to Protestant England to read these encyclicals. You'll find them quite interesting."

The practice of occasionally censoring papal, and frequently censoring episcopal utterances still persists, and there are many other points on which the Church and the Falange are at variance, as for instance the triumphal arch at the entrance of Madrid.

"We do not like", a priest said to me, "an arch to celebrate the victory of Spaniards over Spaniards. We understand that there had to be *one* victory march but to repeat this march every year merely keeps open the wounds of the Civil War."

How I agreed with him! The only fitting Civil War memorial is the Cross near the Escorial on which is inscribed, so I am told, a request for prayers, prayers for tne souls of all who died in that sad fratricidal strife.

XVI

"LEST WE FORGET"

At the end of one of my lectures in America an indignant Catholic rose from the body of the hall and asked me to explain why his Government had withdrawn its ambassadors from Franco and was lending money to Tito.

"They are both dictators but why insult the Catholic dictator and subsidise the atheist dictator?"

"Have you written to your Congressman?" I asked.

"No," he replied.

"Or to your Senator?"

"I'm afraid not."

"*That's* why your Government subsidises an atheist and insults a Catholic dictator."

Roosevelt said that there is no such thing as a Catholic vote. Catholics broadly speaking voted according to their income brackets. Nothing could have been less politically effective than Catholics in the free world when the fate of great Catholic countries was being decided at Yalta and later at Potsdam. It has been argued that it was only right and proper to give Russia a chance to prove that she was capable of a policy of friendly co-operation but was there any evidence to suggest that Stalin had changed? Did not all the available evidence compel us to believe that Stalin remained what he had always been, a ruthless, bloody-minded tyrant whose signature on a document was as worthless as his verbal professions of good will? Had we forgotten the blackest act of treachery in the whole history of war, when Stalin called upon the underground Poles in Warsaw to rise against the Germans and then deliberately halted his armies at the gates of Warsaw? The British and Americans were anxious to fly over Warsaw and drop supplies to the Poles, and to land behind the Russian lines to refuel. Stalin refused the necessary permission. He deliberately delayed his own entry into Warsaw to give his enemies, the Germans, the opportunity to liquidate his allies the Poles. He feared that the Polish underground, who had fought with such heroic gallantry against the Germans, would, after Poland had been annexed by Russia, prove no less heroic in their resistance to Communist tyranny. It was all the more indecent for the Allies to acquiesce in the surrender of Poland to a Communist dictator because throughout the War they had so often proclaimed with sonorous rhetoric their devotion to democracy and their detestation of tyranny.

I know that throughout 1943 the Russians were busily circulating rumours of negotiations in Sweden with the representatives of the Nazis, and that we felt it necessary to bribe them by undertakings which aggravated the admitted difficulties of helping Poland, but the fact that we believed Stalin capable of such treachery should have reinforced our determination to ensure the freedom and independence of our ally.

Towards the end of 1944 I was present at a cocktail party given by a colleague of mine in an organization of which I had been a member. The Rumanian expert in this organization, who had played an important role in the *coup d'état* which eliminated the Nazi sympathisers in Rumania, asked me to dine with him.

"I'm feeling very depressed," he said, "and I want you to cheer me up. I'm going to tell you what I think is going to happen in Europe during the next few years, and I want you to prove me a pessimist."

He then predicted the annexation of Poland, the transformation of Rumania, Hungary, Bulgaria into Communist satellites, and the eventual incorporation of Czechoslovakia into the Communist empire. I had no cure for his pessimism for I agreed with everything which he said. His pessimism was in general shared by Catholics. In general, for there were exceptions.

In 1944 I gave a talk to the Wiseman Society, a somewhat conservative Catholic institution, on the shape of things to come. The chairman rebuked me in no uncertain terms for my lack of faith in Stalin, and I remember a well-known Catholic remarking that he did so hope that Catholics would not allow themselves to be manœuvred into an anti-Russian attitude.

In 1944 those Englishmen who were uneasy about Poland were usually unwilling to discuss the subject, for like Samuel Butler's friend, "They hadn't much conscience and what they had was guilty." And because they were disturbed by occasional doubts, they were all the more eager to insist that everything would work out all right, if only the fanatics did not rock the boat. "Trust Churchill . . .", "Trust Roosevelt . . .", "Don't embarrass the Government", were the slogans evolved to tranquillize uneasy consciences. Catholics were in the main less determined to believe that "Uncle Joe" meant well, but in this wretched climate of selfish appeasement, those responsible for the formation of Catholic opinion fought a desperate rearguard action. The Catholic Press had no illusions about Russia.

The Sword of the Spirit issued a series of excellent pamphlets urging justice for Poland, and the Catholic Hierarchy gave an admirable lead to the Catholic laity, a lead which the informed minority did their best to follow.

Unfortunately Cabinet Ministers are seldom influenced by the pronouncements of bishops or by editorials in religious papers. Democracy is a system of government by rival pressure groups, and Catholics do not constitute a political pressure group. There were a few M.P.s, both Catholic and Protestant, who continued to protest in the House of Commons against the base betrayal of Poland, but the Catholic politicians as a whole were inarticulate. It is not easy for politicians in a democracy to be far ahead of public opinion and as there was no concerted attempt by Catholics to bring pressure to bear on their M.P.s one can hardly blame these M.P.s for being reluctant to risk their political future on an issue about which so few Catholic voters troubled to make their views known to their own M.P.s.

The basic error of the free world was to believe that generous sentiments could take the place of generous actions, that it was enough to express our detestation of tyranny and genocide, but *how much* do we hate these things? *How much* do we care? Are we ready to make the sacrifices which are necessary if the tide of tyranny is to be halted?

In 1936 all nations were present at the Olympic Games in Nazi Germany. Admittedly we knew nothing then of the horrors of German concentration camps, and did not even guess the shape of genocide to come, but racial and religious persecution had begun. I hated everything for which the Nazis stood, but I did not hate Nazism enough to stay away from the Games which had crowned my long campaign by including downhill and slalom ski races for the first time in the Olympic programme, the Games in which my son was captaining the British team. Obviously had I stayed away, this solitary gesture would have had no effect, but the right thing to do remains the right thing to do even if it proves ineffective.

But supposing the free world had boycotted the Games, what then?

"Hitler's position in 1936", a German who had from the first been a bitter opponent of Nazism assured me, "was strong but not yet secure. He would have been terribly weakened by a world boycott of the Olympic Games. The secret opposition had not lost heart. If the world had declared that they could not hold the Games in a country whose Government was treating with contempt the basic laws of civilized and humane behaviour, Hitler's prestige in Germany would have suffered a very sharp decline. The Germans would have realised that the free world meant business, and the War might very well have been avoided. But when we found that the very people who set such store by civilized standards, English aristocrats, for instance, were prepared to accept the hospitality of thugs like Goering, we lost heart. What was the use of our putting our necks in a noose to fight Nazism if the important people on the Olympic Committee were prepared to come to terms with Hitler?"

My own experience with the Nazis convinced me that a boycott of the Games would have had an immense effect. In 1928 I founded with Hannes Schneider the Arlberg-Kandahar ski race which became the Blue Ribbon for Alpine racing. In 1938 the Nazis marched into Austria and imprisoned Hannes Schneider a few days before the Arlberg-Kandahar was due to be held. The Kandahar Ski Club promptly cancelled the event. In the course of the year a number of important Germans wrote to me, including the *Reichssportführer*, urging a resumption of the race in St. Anton.

The British win few Olympic medals, but victory is not the only criterion of status in sport. That we sometimes win international events, and that we invented most of the best games, is less important than the fact that we set a standard of behaviour and formulated the code of sportsmanship. In my own sport, for instance, we revolutionized competitive ski-ing by codifying the rules for downhill racing and by the invention of the slalom, but the effect of our refusal to hold the Arlberg-Kandahar competition under the Nazi flag owed even more to the fact that we stood for certain principles in sport. As the President of the Swiss University Ski Club said of the British pioneers of downhill ski racing: "Their conception of sport was much more developed than ours, clarified through an age-long tradition . . . We learned the meaning of a good loser, of the man who loses with a smile. We learned the meaning of fair play, almost a novelty for us, for which we have no synonym in our mother language."

If, then, British athletes had made it clear, as the Kandahar Ski Club made it clear, that the Nazis were not the sort of people whom we wished to meet in sport, Hitler's prestige would certainly have suffered severely with his own people.

Mutatis mutandis the same is true of Russia to-day. Mr. G. A. Tokaev, the Russian author of *The Betrayal of an Ideal* and perhaps the most important defector from Soviet Russia, assures us that when foreign statesmen began to visit Russia, "these visits were a mortal blow to the democratic opposition within the U.S.S.R.". A diplomat who had spent three years in one of the satellite countries said to me: "If our diplomats never went beyond the limits of the minimum required, if all contacts were cold and formal, if cultural relations were reduced to a minimum, and if, above all, Russians were treated as pariahs in the world of sport, their position with their own people would be undermined. The intellectuals in Russia are already alienated from the régime, there is unrest among the students, but every movement of appeasement in the West discourages the opposition in Russia."

My experience with the Russians confirms the accuracy of these views. In 1949 the Russians applied for admission to the Fédération Internationale de Ski, usually referred to as the F.I.S. Among the conditions which they attempted to impose was the expulsion of the Spanish Ski Association. I persuaded the governing body to rule this impudent proposal out of order, but the President of the F.I.S., instead of carrying out the instructions of his council, allowed not only the Russians but also the Czechs, Bulgarians, Rumanians and Jugoslavs to deliver long political harangues denouncing the Spaniards. In brief, the Russians defied the ruling of the Council, and when a Russian was subsequently elected to the Council I resigned because I did not choose to belong to governing bodies which did not govern. There were no British at the next F.I.S. Congress, a fact which everybody, including the Russians, regretted. The Russians indeed were shrewd enough to realize that their own position was weakened rather than strengthened by the fact that the British had boycotted the Congress, and they even suggested to the Vice-President that I should be formally invited to rejoin the Committee.

We returned to the F.I.S. when a new president was elected, and I was invited, with the cordial support of the Russians, to referee the Slalom at the Olympic Games in 1952. At a F.I.S. banquet, at which I was present as a guest, I made a friendly reference to the Russian on the Committee, a fine ski jumper and from all accounts a decent chap, and explained that my opposition to his election had not been actuated by personal antagonism. My few words were translated by an interpreter and the Russian left his seat, moved round to where I was sitting, carrying two glasses of vodka, placed one glass in front of me, made an eloquent speech about my services to ski-ing and then drank a toast in vodka to my health.

It is a little difficult to understand why Hungary should have made such a profound impression on a world which had managed to forget the even greater horrors which the rulers of Soviet Russia had perpetrated on Poland, the Baltic States and on their own people.

I was in America during the Hungarian revolt. When the last desperate resistance had been crushed in blood, the Diplomatic Corps were invited to a party at the Russian Embassy to celebrate the anniversary of the Bolshevik Revolution. Every guest as he entered the Embassy saw an illuminated cross blazing from the walls of the C.I.O. Headquarters, the Temple of American Labour. Underneath that cross were the words: "REMEMBER THE HUNGARIAN MARTYRS." The Russians rang up the State Department, and the police came round and asked the Labour officials to remove the cross and the offending words, but these men stood their ground and refused to remove the cross excepting as the result of a court order, knowing well that no such court order could be obtained till next day.

Switzerland was so deeply moved that the Swiss forgot their tradition of neutrality. The Rector of Berne University had, as usual, invited the Diplomatic Corps to the *Dies Academicus* at which honorary degrees are conferred. The students went in a body to the Rector and informed him that unless the invitations to the Russian diplomats were cancelled, not one student would attend the *Dies Academicus*. The invitation was withdrawn.

A nationwide demonstration was organized. At an appointed time every factory stopped working and trains and trams halted. From Lindau to Lugano, from Geneva to Buchs, church bells tolled. Men and women stood in silence, and those who still pray prayed for the liberation of Hungary and the overthrow of the Russian tyrants.

The repercussions in the world of sport were no less significant. Some nations declined to send teams to Melbourne as they refused to compete against the Russians. The Dutch withdrew their team and gave the money subscribed for the team to Hungarian refugees. The Swiss cancelled their entry but had second thoughts too late to book a plane, and were not represented. The only Swiss in the team who had won a gold medal at the previous Olympics had no second thoughts. He made it clear that nothing would induce him to meet the Russians in sport.

At the beginning of the winter Herr G. Michel, President of the Swiss Ski Association, sent a courteous but firm letter to the Russians suggesting that it would be better if no Russians competed in Swiss ski-ing events such as the Lauberhorn Cup or the S.D.S. at Grindelwald. There were no Russians at Holmenkollen, once again as the result of courteous representations from their hosts.

In the summer of 1957 I met M. Paul Morand, a former President of the Swiss Gymnastic Association, who assured me that the Swiss gymnasts had firmly maintained their refusal to compete in any event in which the Russians are competing until such time as they withdraw their armies from the satellites.

Those Swiss realised that generous sentiments cost nothing, and that the only effective protests in the modern world are those made by people who are prepared to make real sacrifices to prove the sincerity of their convictions, such as for instance sacrificing a free trip to Australia for the Olympic Games.

Obviously a price must be paid; if we refused to meet the Russians in sport we should be penalising Russians who were not responsible for the crimes of their Government, but inevitably the innocent suffer with the guilty in all forms of human conflict. Many a woman and child was killed by bombs in Germany and atom bombs in Japan. It has also been argued that such contacts with Russian athletes may weaken their allegiance to Communism. I can assess the value of such contacts for I spent the Olympic week in February 1956 in the Tre Croci Hotel at Cortina, which was the headquarters of the Russian team.

It is exceptional for a Russian athlete to speak any language but Russian, a fact which in itself renders social contacts all but impossible. The only visitor in the hotel who did speak Russian had begun to talk to some members of the Russian team when a middle-aged Russian, perhaps one of the Secret Police who were known to be accompanying the team, sat down between them.

Again, if we refused to meet the Russians in sport they would, of course, explain our attitude by the fear that we could not hope to beat them, and certainly the Olympic Games would lose something of its prestige if many of the world's greatest athletes were excluded. But once more it is a question of priorities. What matters most to us—our vanity, which might suffer from Russian jibes, the prestige of some great event such as the Olympic Games which enhances the importance both of officials and competitors, or the possibility, if only the faint possibility, of helping the oppressed?

At a time when the last flicker of Hungarian freedom was being extinguished by Russian tanks, I saw a press photograph of British and American athletes at the Melbourne Olympics exchanging broad smiles with Russian athletes. There are some things even more important than the prestige of sport, a sense of decency, that is, a sense of what is or what is not fitting.

XVII

"THE PERFUME OF AN EMPTY VASE"

SIXTY years ago I watched the great Queen ride past to give thanks at St. Paul's for her sixty years on the throne. Only those who are old enough to remember the confident certainties of the Victorian age can fully appreciate the contrast with the climate of anxiety in which we are living today. I wonder if even Kipling himself took his *Recessional* seriously,

> Lord God of Hosts be with us yet
> Lest we forget, lest we forget.

The dominant philosophy of the nineteenth century was "Dawnism", a word coined by my brother, the late Hugh Kingsmill. Dawnism is the philosophy of those who believe that the rosy dawn of a new day is imminent, a new day in which the troubles of the individual will be solved by some form of collective action. Even Christians who should have known better were infected by Dawnism. Even Catholics were not wholly convinced by papal warnings, as for instance by passages such as these in Leo XIII's *Rerum Novarum* (1891):

> If any there be who pretend differently—who hold out to a hard-pressed people the boon of freedom from pain and trouble, an undisturbed repose, and constant enjoyment—they delude the people and impose upon

> them, and their lying promises will one day bring forth worse evils than the present. Nothing is more useful than to look upon the world as it really is.

And nothing is rarer in Dawnist circles.

"In times of shallow optimism," wrote a great agnostic, Leslie Stephen, "the profounder spirits are pessimistic." Those whose judgement on this world, and on the shape of secular things to come, was a conclusion from the austere premisses of Christian teaching, were uninfected by Dawnism. I remember a September evening in 1940 when the sky above London was red with reflection of flames, and the heavens criss-crossed by searchlights hunting for the dark invader; I found myself repeating the famous passage with which Ruskin opens *The Stones of Venice*.

> Since first the dominion of men was asserted over the ocean, three thrones, of mark beyond all others, have been set upon its sands: the thrones of Tyre, Venice, and England. Of the first of these great powers only the memory remains; of the second, the ruin; the third which inherits their greatness, if it forget their example, may be led through prouder eminence to less pitied destruction.

"It is no exaggeration", wrote Renan in the first enthusiasm of his conversion to Dawnism, "to say that science contains the future of humanity, and that it alone can say the last word on human destiny and teach mankind how to reach its goal." Thanks to science, humanity may have no future, for the hydrogen bomb may prove to be the "last word on human destiny". Whereas in the nineties many an idealist scientist could console himself for the loss of all hope of personal immortality by his faith in the power of science to usher in a new dawn, no such Utopian illusions are possible today. "Progress", wrote Herbert Spencer, a Victorian Dawnist, "is not an accident but a necessity. What we call evil and immorality must disappear. It is certain that man must become perfect." What agnostic would dare to write like that today?

The years which Renan spent in a seminary before he apostatized were not wholly wasted. The influences of Catholic rationalism, even after he had left the Church, finally cured him of the illusions of Dawnism.

> It seems possible [he wrote] that the collapse of supernatural belief will be followed by the collapse of moral convictions, and that the moment when humanity sees the reality of things will mark a real moral decline ... We are living on the perfume of an empty vase.

Even the perfume has faded today.

Time (12 August, 1957) contains a sickening story of murder by one of the many gangs of teenagers which infest New York. "The Egyptian Kings", as this particular gang was called, had lost a game of "stickball" to "The Jesters" and had refused to pay a fifty-cent bet on the game. Infuriated by the protests of "The Jesters", they decided on revenge. Seventeen members of the gang waylaid at night two boys whom they believed, erroneously, to belong to "The Jesters", and slashed them with knives. Mike Farmer was killed. A fourteen-year-old boy known to his pals as "The Little King" proudly bragged to detectives that he had plunged his knife deep into Farmer's back "to get the feeling of a knife going through the bone". As he withdrew the blade he said to the dying boy: "Thanks a lot." "One night, only seventy-three hours after the Farmer attack, eighteen-year-old George

Marshall, standing on a Bronx street with a friend, was set upon by five boys and two girls, and stabbed to death as his companions ran for help. As the headlines blossomed fearful mothers pulled their children from parks..."

A friend of mine in New York told me that it would be madness to walk across Central Park at night. A few days before a woman had been raped in Central Park before it was dark.

In England it is fashionable to explain such horrors as the result of war and the evacuation of children from bombed areas. No doubt the war aggravated existing tendencies, but Renan was right. The collapse of supernatural belief has been followed by a real moral decline. Moral nihilism has been aggravated by the fear that the planet itself is doomed. Thucydides' description of Athens during the great plague has a certain relevance to the world in which we live.

> As both their bodies and their wealth seemed to them to be transitory they were determined to seize any pleasures which were easily available and to satisfy their lusts . . . they were unrestrained by the fear of gods or law of men; for since all men were perishing alike, it seemed to them that the consequences of piety and impiety were the same, as nobody expected to live long enough to be punished for his crimes. On the contrary they believed that the penalty which awaited them was far heavier, and that it was rational to extract enjoyment of life before they met their doom.

Many years before the first atom bomb had been dropped, Hilaire Belloc noted "the rising tide of despair", and long before his conversion to Christianity Cyril Joad commented on the coincidence between the decline of religion and the rising suicide rate.

No Dawnist was more confident than H. G. Wells that the key to Utopia was to replace the priest by the scientist, or more disillusioned when this experiment was tried out in Soviet Russia. He watched with dismay not one but scores of Russian Galileos persecuted because their scientific beliefs did not coincide with Marxist dogmas.

"Science" is a Latin word which means knowledge, and knowledge is morally neutral. It can be used either for good or evil. I am not by any means convinced that the invention of the atom bomb was a disaster. At Yalta and Potsdam we were prepared to concede almost all that Stalin could reasonably have expected to be given, and if it had not been for the deterrent of the atom bomb Russia today would be the master of Europe.

I can understand that Dawnists should be disillusioned, but I am puzzled by the fact that many Christians seem to feel that the invention of the atom bomb has created new difficulties of belief. The problem of moral evil and physical pain is unchanged by recent developments which, if anything, should reinforce rather than weaken the faith of a Christian. It is not we but the Dawnists who find it difficult to reconcile the threat of unimaginable horrors with their Utopian philosophy. There is nothing Dawnist about the New Testament. Our Lord never promised his followers an easy time or predicted that wars would end. Read the twenty-fourth chapter of St. Matthew: "And you will hear tell of wars, and rumours of wars; see to it that you are not disturbed in mind"—not even by rumours of the atom bomb: "Such things must happen, but the end will not come yet. Nation will rise in arms against nation, kingdom against kingdom, and there will be plagues and famine, and earthquakes in this region or that; *but all this is but the beginning of travail.*" No hint of a rosy dawn in these words of our Lord.

Recent history should reinforce rather than weaken the

faith of Christians. We profess to believe that unless the Lord build the house, they labour in vain that build it, but the Lord is not even consulted in our plans for the building of a new world. God was left out of the League of Nations. There was not one religious symbol in the building. God was left out of U.N.O. We spent the war years denouncing religious persecution and dictatorships. We began the war to save Poland from one dictator and we ended the war by selling Poland down the river to another dictator. We have done nothing effectively to protest against the continuance of religious persecution in Russia or Red China. There was no principle which we were not prepared to sacrifice if only we could guarantee peace and prosperity for ourselves. If by this means we could have exorcised war and rendered Communism innocuous, the atheist could claim with some justice that it is safe to ignore God, but God is not mocked, and if and when an atom-bomb war breaks out, the Christian at least will know what is hitting him and why it is hitting him, but the poor Utopians will have no such consolation.

XVIII

"THE CONQUEST OF HAPPINESS"

It is the exceptional sceptic who has the courage to face the logical consequences of his beliefs. Bertrand Russell must therefore be given credit for refusing to evade the consequences of a philosophy which denies the supernatural.

> That man [writes Russell] is the product of causes which had no prevision of the end they were achieving; that his origin, his growth, his hopes and fears, his loves and his beliefs, are but the outcome of accidental collocations of atoms; that no fire, no heroism, no intensity of thought and feeling, can preserve an individual life beyond the grave; that all the labour of the ages, all the devotion, all the inspiration, all the noonday brightness of human genius are destined to extinction in the vast death of the solar system, and that the whole temple of man's achievement must inevitably be buried beneath the debris of a universe in ruins—all these things, if not quite beyond dispute, are yet so nearly certain, that no philosophy which rejects them can hope to stand. Only within the scaffolding of these truths, only on the firm foundation of unyielding despair, can the soul's habitation henceforth be safely built.

Nothing, however, is more difficult than for a sceptic to be consistent. If man's "loves and beliefs" are but the outcome of an "accidental collocation of atoms" then our beliefs are the by-product of forces alien to reason and are therefore not the result of any rational process. We have, therefore, no means of knowing whether in fact our beliefs *are* the "outcome of accidental collocations of atoms". Bertrand Russell, in fact, is busily engaged in sawing away the branch on which he is sitting, for the only rational consequence of accepting materialism is the suspicion that we have no rational grounds for accepting any belief, including materialism. And clearly, if all our beliefs are predetermined, it is rubbish to discuss what should be a "free man's worship", for man on this hypothesis is not free.

Moreover, if no philosophy which rejects these alleged truths of materialism "can hope to stand", what precisely does Lord Russell mean by the "soul" whose habitation must be based on the firm foundation of unyielding despair? And if all our hopes and our beliefs and our ethical standards are the product of material forces which are alien to morality, what precisely is the "free" man expected to worship? This pose of heroic despair would be more convincing if we were not reminded of Samuel Johnson's friend, Edwards. "I have tried too in my time", said Edwards, "to be a philosopher, but, I don't know how, cheerfulness was always breaking in."

It was, I suppose, the irruptions of cheerfulness which were responsible for Bertrand Russell's book *The Conquest of Happiness*, but it is a little difficult to understand how the "free man", having carried out Lord Russell's instructions to build his soul's habitation on the firm foundations of unyielding despair, can then proceed to master the technique of conquering happiness. It is perhaps rather pedantic to dissect a passage, the charm of which is due not to exact reasoning but to rhetoric. As Keats remarks in a somewhat different connection:

Do not all charms fly
At the mere touch of cold philosophy?

The title of Bertrand Russell's book, *The Conquest of Happiness*, suggests a misconception of the very nature of happiness, for happiness is not something one conquers; on the contrary it is the by-product of self-conquest. "There is still the old source of strength," says Rachel Quarles, a character in one of Aldous Huxley's novels, "old but not dull. There is nothing less dull than God. But most people won't believe me when I tell them so, even though they are bored to death with jazz bands and dancing. They are on the wrong road. If people asked how can we please God, and why aren't we better, they would achieve happiness without even thinking of it."

Happiness cannot be conquered. It must be earned and the price to be paid is the sacrifice of some pleasures as every ascetic fully realises. Whereas the Puritan condemns the pleasures of which he disapproves as wicked, the ascetic abstains from pleasures which he knows to be innocent as the price which he must pay for the higher forms of happiness. An ascetic may drink nothing but water, but he does not lapse into the heresy of Puritanism unless he condemns those who drink wine. Pleasure and happiness are not identical. An Oxford undergraduate was asked in an examination paper to comment on Aristotle's dictum, "A good man can be happy on the rack." He replied, "Possibly, if it was a very bad rack or if he was a very good man." Good men have been happy even on good racks for, as that puzzled pagan Seneca observed, men have been known to laugh and "that right heartily" under torture. One may cite as a modern example of happiness in spite of acute suffering the death of the Catholic martyrs in Uganda, pages of the king Mwanga, on the Feast of the Assumption, 1883.

> There were no screams of pain coming from the burning pages, only the sounds of their prayers, their voices

quite normal, growing softer and softer until the last boy died. The executioners could not believe what their eyes saw. They stood there quietly, stunned, afraid, until the flames finally flickered out.[1]

This ascetic principle explains the spell of the hard sports, mountaineering for instance. The mountaineer sacrifices the legitimate pleasure of a night in bed for a night in a tent or overcrowded club hut, or beneath the stars. He pays for his happiness by fatigue and often by fear. The horror of a half-slip when leading on an exposed climb, the desperate struggle to regain balance, a struggle which is a matter of small readjustments on a battleground measured in inches, are the price which the cragsman pays for the quasi-mystical happiness of those moments when his mind has asserted its mastery over the body, when the effortless rhythm of the upward movements transforms the accident of crack and ledge into an ordered sequence of harmonious movement. I was never more aware of the contrast between happiness and pleasure than during an attempt on Mont Blanc in my sixty-eighth year, an attempt which failed owing to a storm which drove me back from the summit of the Aiguille du Goûter (12,582 ft.). From the time that I started to the time when I returned there had not been one pleasurable moment, for I had been too tired to sleep in the overcrowded huts, and my game leg gave me a lot of trouble, but even on the most wearying parts of the climb there had been flashes of that queer ascetic happiness which rewards the conquest of exhaustion and pain.

The flight from asceticism explains much which would otherwise be puzzling in modern philosophy. The hope that those who have been defeated by the flesh can conquer happiness is the key to the fake objectivity of the new

[1] *The White Fathers*, by Glen D. Kittler, London, W. H. Allen, p. 196.

morality. In their attempt to formulate an objective code to justify subjective weaknesses these apostles of hedonism often appeal to the bogus Hellenism of Goethe, who contrasted the happy uninhibited Greeks with the victims of the "destructive Christian doctrine of sin". The impression which these neo-Hellenists try to convey is, as I have elsewhere maintained, "that they have read a great deal of Greek history and philosophy before arriving at certain academic conclusions on the subject of sex, and that they have recorded these with the academic detachment of a eunuch. I far prefer the honesty of Oscar Wilde—'The only way to get rid of temptations is to yield to them.'"

That the pursuit of pleasure renders impossible the achievement of happiness is a truth which our generation is beginning to suspect. The same factors which made possible the triumph of Christianity in the pagan world are in operation today. Even Jung, the famous psychologist, for all his prejudice against Christianity could write:

> At a time when a large part of mankind is beginning to discard Christianity it is worth while to understand clearly why it was originally accepted. It was accepted to escape at last from the brutality of antiquity. As soon as we discard it, licentiousness returns. . . . The meaning of Christianity and Mithraism is clear. It is a moral restraint of animal impulses. The dynamic appearance of both religions betrays something of that enormous feeling of redemption which animated the first disciples and which we today scarcely know how to appreciate. Those old truths are empty to us. Most certainly we should still understand them had our customs even a breath of ancient brutality, for we can hardly realise in this day the whirlwinds of the unchained libido which roared through the ancient Rome of the Caesars.

Even in the days when the late C. E. M. Joad was not only an agnostic but hostile to institutional Christianity he was intelligent enough to suspect a certain connection between the decline of religion and the increase of unhappiness. In his book *The Present and Future of Religion*, written in the late 'twenties, he wrote:

> For the first time in history there is coming to maturity a generation of men and women who have no religion, and feel no need for one. They are content to ignore it. Also they are very unhappy, and the suicide rate is abnormally high.

Again, in the 1932 issue of *To-day and To-morrow*, this enlightened agnostic wrote:

> It is notorious that heavenly rewards no longer attract and infernal punishments no longer deter with their pristine force; young people are frankly derisive of both, and seeing no prospect of divine compensation in the next world for the wine and kisses that morality bids them eschew in this one, take more or less unanimously to the wine and kisses. Unfortunately the pleasurable results anticipated from these sources fail to materialise. That unchecked indulgence in the more obvious types of pleasure is unsatisfying, is the unanimous teaching of those who have had the leisure and opportunity to try them in all ages. It is the more unfortunate that it is a truth which nobody believes to be true until he has discovered it for himself. . . . You cannot take the kingdom of pleasure, any more than you can take the kingdom of beauty, by storm.

In brief, happiness cannot be conquered. It can only be earned.

Happiness is admittedly partly a question of temperament. There are convinced believers who seem less happy than carefree hedonists. Hilaire Belloc, for instance, was a man of strong faith but he never wholly recovered from the death of his wife, and of his son Louis in action. His autumn years were saddened by the collapse of his beloved France in 1940. But the Faith, if it did not save Belloc from melancholy, certainly saved him from despair, and there is no convinced Christian who could not make his own a sentence from his famous letter to Dean Inge:

> Even in these our earthly miseries we always hear the distant something of an eternal music, and smell a native air.

Hilaire Belloc was depressed by what he somewhere calls "the awful brevity of life", for a man may be a convinced Catholic and yet not find it easy to reconcile himself to declining powers and to approaching age. "The change from progress to decadence", wrote Lord Melbourne to Queen Victoria, "is a very hard and disagreeable trial—Lord Melbourne has been reading Cicero on old age, a very pretty treatise, but he does not find much consolation in it." Nor did I when I recently reread *De Senectute*. The sentiments are irreproachable, as, for instance, *ex vita discendo tamquam ex hospitio, non tamquam e domo*, but one can agree with Cicero that one should be prepared to leave life "as if it were an inn, not a home", and yet recall with a certain nostalgia one's early memories of this most congenial inn. I found nothing in Cicero, or for that matter in other moralists who have discussed old age—Seneca and Epictetus, for instance—which consoled me for the fact that I can no longer climb and that my power to work is slowly failing.

In my sixty-eighth year I wrote two books, of which *A Century of Mountaineering* involved a great deal of reading, edited and wrote about fifteen thousand words for *The British Ski Year Book*, wrote some seventy-five articles, including a weekly article, and did a three-months lecture tour in America. Only two years have passed since then, but I find it increasingly difficult to sit down to my typewriter after dinner. Yet though I cannot offer my elderly readers any Ciceronian consolations, it seems to me slightly unfair that I should criticise other people's recipes for happiness and yet prudently refrain from exposing myself to similar criticisms by the reader. I will therefore make my own modest contribution to the problem of happiness. Here is my formula. "You can avoid unnecessary unhappiness by refusing to dwell on dead options." I can illustrate what I mean by quoting a comment by a friend on something I had said. I had happened to remark that it was exasperating to suffer a crippling accident at the beginning of a mountaineering career. Phyllis Holt-Needham said, "I've never heard you make a remark like that before." True enough, because it only makes me unhappy to allow my mind to dwell on "dead options". Instead, I feel profoundly grateful for the fact that though I never led a difficult rock climb since my accident it was not until my sixty-eighth year that I climbed my last big peak. The fact that I still have two legs I owe, under God, to the courageous decision of one of my greatest friends, C. Scott Lindsay, and I should like to take this opportunity to quote from a recent article of his by way of putting on record my gratitude.

> At about 11 o'clock that night, when the rescue party were approaching Dolgelly with Arnold on a stretcher, I met them on the road to find him conscious but lucid, though in great pain. His first words were "Do you

think I shall ever climb again?" A grim sequel to that question soon pressed upon me at about 2 a.m. next morning. In the hotel at Dolgelly in which we had improvised an operating table, Dick Warren the surgeon, who was to do his best for him, came to me with a grave expression on his face to say that in view of the dirty state of the wound, and of the time which had elapsed since the fall, it was strictly his duty to amputate the leg on account of the danger of gangrene. And that he could only fail to amputate if a third party, responsible to the family, were to ask him to do so. [My parents were on a cruise.] It did not take me long to reflect that Arnold without a leg would find life intolerable, and that the risk should be taken, and I gave Dick Warren the reply he sought. The luck was with both of us, but at twenty-one the decision was not easy to make.

I am convinced that a resolute refusal to allow one's mind to dwell on might-have-beens—in my case the possibility of being selected for an Everest expedition—saves one from a great deal of unnecessary brooding. The dismissing from one's mind of dead options does not, of course, eliminate the inevitable regrets as one's powers decline, but long before I became a Catholic I was impressed by the serene happiness of many elderly people, whom I knew to be fortified against the fear of death by the hope of that happiness which God has prepared for those that love him, and I could not help contrasting their happiness with that pagan sadness which was expressed with inimitable felicity by Horace and Catullus and which finds less attractive expression in the rootless art and literature of modern secularism. It is difficult for an intelligent sceptic to achieve anything more satisfactory than stoic acquiescence as death approaches.

It is certainly easier for an atheist to be happy in his youth and middle years than in the twilight of his life.

Compare, for instance, H. G. Wells in his middle years —"The life to which I belong uses me and will pass on beyond me and I am content"—with Wells reduced to despair by the imminence of death: "A frightful queerness has come into life. . . . There is no way out of or round or through the impasse. It is the end . . . the attempt to trace a pattern of any sort is absolutely futile. . . . The present writer has no compelling argument to convince the reader that he should not be cruel or mean or cowardly." I have taken this quotation from Wells' testament of despair, *Mind at the End of its Tether*.

I remember a similar evolution from apparent contentment to despair in the case of a friend of mine who was rich, successful and well pleased with life in his middle years. He suffered no pain and was not confined to bed in his last weeks but he died without hope, and never have I seen despair more tragically apparent than in the expression on my friend's face when we last met.

If man's life be nothing but a flicker of consciousness between the womb and the tomb, unredeemed from futility by any ultimate significance, there is no escape from the sadness of pagan antiquity, the sadness of Catullus, as expressed in the well-known lines: "Suns may set and rise, but when once our brief light has faded, we must sleep the sleep of the unending night."

Soles occidere et redire possunt;
Nobis cum semel occidit brevis lux
Nox est perpetua, una, dormienda.

I suspect that many of those who argued in favour of atheism and materialism had their moments when they doubted their doubts.

Just when we're safest, there's a sunset touch
A fancy from a flower-bell, someone's death,
A chorus-ending from Euripides,—
And that's enough for fifty hopes and fears
As old and new at once as Nature's self,
To rap and knock and enter in our soul.

Nobody who adores beauty in any one of her many manifestations can fail to doubt the dogmatic negations of the materialist, for every lover of beauty must be influenced consciously or unconsciously by the doctrine that beauty in its many manifestations is a reflection of the eternal beauty which time cannot corrupt. John Tyndall, for instance, was often regarded as an exponent of a scientific materialism, but in his 1874 address to the British Association he insisted that "it is not in hours of clearness or self-vigour that this doctrine commends itself to my mind". On the contrary, the doctrines of materialism "dissolved in the presence of stronger and healthier thought as offering no solution to the mystery in which we dwell". It may have been the mountains which provoked the antidote of "healthier thought", the mountains in whose beauty this great agnostic saw reflections of a beauty which he hesitated to recognize as divine. "Some people", Tyndall said to Newman Hall, "give me little credit for religious feeling. I assure you that when I walk here and gaze at these mountains I am filled with adoration."

It was the mountains which led me, as they had led Tyndall, away from the arid desert of materialism.

I was nineteen at the time. I was just returning from a glorious day among the mountains. The rope had been discarded and we were smoking a quiet pipe on a little pass a few thousand feet above the valley plunged in the rich gloom of an Alpine twilight.

The evening breeze served as a soft pedal to the music of a glacier stream which faded into *piano* when the wind rose. Sixty miles away the white bar of the Oberland snows saluted the setting sun. The golden glow of evening subdued the strong lines of the mountains, and confused the issue of separate and successive slopes. A white speck that was Chillon showed against the purple of the lake. The whole vast shadowed landscape seemed to be haunted by an all-pervading sense of something of which visible beauty was only the sacramental expression. I thought of Haeckel's dusty nonsense and laughed aloud. And from that moment I discarded materialism for ever.[1]

That Alpine sunset on the Col de Breya was the first clue which was to lead me after many years to the Seven Hills. I had been a young man with two legs of approximately the same length when I last crossed the Col de Breya; I was in my seventieth year when I took the new lift from the lovely Lac Champex to the Col and scrambled up on to the little hillock overlooking the pass.

Two young men with rope and axe had just left the pass and were making their way towards the Cabane D'Orny, where I had slept on the night before I climbed my first Alpine peak. And suddenly all the romance of that early initiation into the adventure of the snows came back to me like stars after a storm, the shadowy silhouette of the peaks against the star-pointed night as we left the hut, the glacier wind which ruffled the silence of the snows, the eastern sky lit by Dante's *splendori antelucani*, the serene happiness of the summit.

If one returns year by year to the places one loved as a boy, the memories of youth mingle with those of maturity and sometimes lose their distinctness, but there was no

[1] *Now I See*, p. 21.

such confusion of recollection on the Col de Breya for it was fifty years since I crossed this pass of many memories.

They say that in the unchanging place
  Where all we loved is always dear
We meet our morning face to face
  And find at last our twentieth year.

To a Greek, or to a modern who has inherited the melancholy of paganism, those moments on the Col de Breya when I met my "morning face to face" would have been dominated with the sadness of mortality. To the Greek all joy was centred in this life and even the golden hours of sunlit youth were darkened by the morbid shadow of death and decay, and unconsoled by the prospect of the only future life in which the Greek believed, a spectral hereafter drained alike of vital joy and sorrow. Mimnermus is in the Greek tradition when he writes "when youth has fled, short-lived as a dream, forthwith this burdensome and ugly old age looms over us, detestable and dishonoured", but on the Col de Breya I was consoled by a certainty which Mimnermus never entertained, the conviction that in those rare moments of perfect felicity which are granted to us on earth there is something which stands outside of time and which is not subject to decay. The serene untroubled happiness of that hour on the Col de Breya was remote not only from the mood of Mimnermus but also from the stoic resignation of Epictetus, however apposite to my state of physical decay might be his famous saying—"What is left for a lame old man but to sing hymns to God?"

No, I was not sad like Mimnermus nor resigned like Epictetus, but serenely content. I looked across the valley to the Doric splendour of the Grand Combin which I had traversed in a snowstorm with my brother Hugh, and instead of mourning my lost youth in the manner of Mimnermus I gave thanks for the mountains among which I had discovered the happiness which is undimmed by age, the happiness which cannot be conquered but which can be earned.

I agree with that distinguished mountaineer Charles Meade that "whatever importance nature mysticism may have in relation to religious mysticism is due to its potentially preparatory character", but I am none the less grateful for the revelation of God in the beauty of the mountains and for those moments among the hills when we enjoy a foretaste of the happiness which will, perhaps, be "our settled state if we deserve or attain beatitude".

INDEX

INDEX

(*The names of saints and popes are grouped together under "Saint" and "Pope" respectively*)

BY THE SAME AUTHOR

GUIDE TO MONTANA (1907)
OXFORD MOUNTAINEERING ESSAYS (*ed.*) (1912)
THE ENGLISHMAN IN THE ALPS (1912)
THE HARROVIANS (1913)
SKI-ING (1913)
THE ALPS (*Home University Library*) (1914)
LOOSE ENDS (1919)
AUCTION PIQUET (*nom-de-plume* Rubicon) (1920)
CROSS-COUNTRY SKI-ING (1920)
THE ALPINE SKI-GUIDE (BERNESE OBERLAND) (1920)
ALPINE SKI-ING (1921)
ROMAN CONVERTS (1924)
SKI-ING FOR BEGINNERS (1924)
THE MOUNTAINS OF YOUTH (1925)
A HISTORY OF SKI-ING (1927)
THINGS THAT HAVE PUZZLED ME (1927)
SWITZERLAND (*Kitbag Travel Books*) (1927)
JOHN WESLEY (1928)
THE FLIGHT FROM REASON (1930)
THE COMPLETE SKI-RUNNER (1930)
FAMILY NAME (1931)
VENICE (*Kitbag Travel Books*) (1932)
(*With Rev. R. A. Knox*) DIFFICULTIES (1932)
THE ITALIAN LAKES AND LAKELAND CITIES (1932)
WITHIN THE PRECINCTS OF THE PRISON (1932)
(*With C. E. M. Joad*) IS CHRISTIANITY TRUE? (1933)
NOW I SEE (1933)
A SAINT IN THE SLAVE TRADE (1934)
(*With Prof. J. B. S. Haldane, F.R.S.*) SCIENCE AND THE SUPERNATURAL (1935)
WITHIN THAT CITY (1936)
SPANISH REHEARSAL (1937)
COMMUNISM AND SOCIALISM (1938)
WHITHER EUROPE? (1940)
COME WHAT MAY: AN AUTOBIOGRAPHY (1940)
AND THE FLOODS CAME (1942)
MOUNTAIN JUBILEE (1943)
THE GOOD GORILLA (1943)
SWITZERLAND AND THE ENGLISH (1944)
THE THIRD DAY (1945)
(*With Dr. G. G. Coulton*) IS THE CATHOLIC CHURCH ANTI-SOCIAL? (1946)
SWITZERLAND IN ENGLISH PROSE AND POETRY (1947)
MOUNTAINS OF MEMORY (1948)
THE REVOLT AGAINST REASON (1950)
THE CRADLE OF SWITZERLAND (1952)
THE STORY OF SKI-ING (1952)
ZERMATT AND THE VALAIS (1955)
MEMORY TO MEMORY (1956)
ENIGMA (1957)
A CENTURY OF MOUNTAINEERING (1957)
THE BERNESE OBERLAND (1958)

This book is dedicated
to the memory of

JOHN F. KENNEDY

FOREWORD

This book presents a comparative study of the root problems of economic growth in each of the three great subdivisions of the contemporary world: the newly developing countries, the Soviet orbit, and the West.

Economic development and growth dominate the thoughts and policies of the contemporary world. The Communist Party Program of November, 1961, based Soviet global designs on its expectations regarding economic development and growth in the newly developing countries, in the Soviet orbit, and in the West. To assess these designs correctly, and to counter them effectively, we must understand clearly the key problems of economic development in each of the three main segments of the world. This is the particular subject and purpose of this study.

The newly developing countries are struggling through the early stages of economic growth. Their economic development is guided typically by deliberate, sometimes arbitrary, political aspirations, which often produce irregular and precarious patterns of growth. The Soviet orbit has attained that stage of development where modern technology is broadly applied to production. Its productive capacity however, which is chiefly oriented toward technological superiority in support of Communist power, falls short of satisfactory levels of consumption. The advanced industrial countries of the West, on the other hand, have developed affluent societies of high mass consumption, even though they experience the pressures of pluralistic institutions and rigidities, relative deficiency of public services, and increasing requirements for defense, foreign aid, and space navigation.

The United States finds itself in a particularly intricate dilemma. Its rate of economic growth has been sluggish for years, with high rates of unemployment and idle industrial capacity. On the other hand, because of its world-wide commitments, the United States has experienced a chronic deficit in its total payments relations with the rest of the world, a situation which has resulted in systematic losses of monetary gold. It is not entirely clear how much of the sluggishness in the American economy is due to technological change and institutional rigidities and how much of it can be blamed directly on the deficiency of the total demand for goods and services. Because of the persistent difficulties concerning the balance of international payments, American monetary and fiscal policies have been cautious lest another upsurge of inflation further aggravate the country's international payments position.

Against the background of such differences, each of the world's three great subdivisions has a particular root problem of its own economic growth. For the newly developing countries, the key problem is not primarily the shortage of capital, but the vast and uneven lag of human skills in production and its organization. Examination of Soviet economic development reveals that the main obstacle is the widening and deepening contradiction between the autocratic management and the pretended socialist character of the Soviet economic system.

Faced with their pluralistic pressures and institutional rigidities, the increasing need for expanded public services, defense, foreign aid, and the space race, the advanced industrial economies of the West in general, and of the United States in particular, must view the constant danger of two-pronged inflation (from the cost and demand sides) as the main difficulty of economic growth. Since vigorous growth-oriented policies can generate inflation as their unintended by-product, fear of inflation may act as a basic obstacle to an otherwise desirable and possible higher rate of growth. If this dilemma, which is particularly acute in the United States, is to be overcome, inflationary pressures from the cost side must first be eliminated or effectively harnessed. This now appears an essential condition for a simultaneous solution to the dual root problem of the American economy.

But the phenomenon of inflation is not limited to the West. Although in the economies of the new nations and the Soviet orbit there are growth problems that are both more basic and more important than inflation, inflationary pressures are a common characteristic of all contemporary economies. Moreover, analysis shows that the key problems of economic growth in the newly developing countries (cultural lag and entrepreneurial lag) and in the Soviet orbit (increasing tension between autocratic management and socialist pressures in the Soviet economy) are closely associated with inflationary tendencies in their economies. Inflation thus assumes a broader significance in the framework of the global problems of economic growth. Inflation is a comprehensive indicator of the existing limitations and of specific obstacles to economic growth in all contemporary economies.

This book examines each of the three distinct root problems of economic growth and seeks ways to their solutions. It also explores the possibility that through solution of these problems the economies of the three main subdivisions may gradually develop increasing similarities.

To put it in more conventional terms, this book may be said to deal with the unresolved problems of interdependence and interplay between economic development and growth on the one hand, and the various social systems of economic organization on the other. That differences in economic systems are bound to influence processes and achievements of economic development and growth has, of course, been admitted all along. However, such differential influences have either been beclouded by ideological squabbles or simply dismissed as subjects unsuitable for economic analysis. This book makes an attempt at clarifying and specifying these influences.

In the course of exploring solutions to the specific problems of economic growth that are found to be inherent in the various economic systems of today, the inverse relationship emerges. When their inherent growth problems are recognized and attacked within each system, the corresponding processes of economic development and growth begin to generate significant "feedback" effects on the economic systems within which they evolve.

In spite of the still great differences among them, the various economic systems in the world today are already showing signs of converging toward greater similarities in their essential functions. This tendency has potential implications that reach far beyond the narrow limits of "economic" welfare alone.

Although organized systematically and presented analytically, the book is written in as nontechnical language as the overriding objective of dependable explanation permits. Some of the shortcomings of this approach are offset by including short appendixes on the more important technical aspects of the subject. It is felt that the potential usefulness of the book will thus be enhanced without impairing its readability. The appendixes may well serve to make the book suitable as a school text in a variety of courses.

I wish to thank all those who have offered assistance in the preparation of this book. Professor William Fellner of Yale read the manuscript and expressed critical evaluation of its several parts. My colleagues, Professors Goetz A. Briefs, Josef Solterer, Gunther Ruff, Henry Briefs, and Stanislas Wasowski read and discussed with me various sections of the manuscript. Special thanks go to Dr. S. Pejovich, who untiringly assisted me throughout the preparation of the book, particularly its many references and appendixes. But I alone am responsible for any shortcomings of the book.

A number of distinguished European economists were of great help to me when I was studying the European aspects of the subject. I am particularly grateful to Professor Erich Schneider and his able staff at the Institut für Weltwirtschaft of the University of Kiel, Professor François Perroux of the Collège de France, Professor Godfried Bombach of the University of Basel, Professor Friedrich Lutz of the University of Zurich, and Professor Francesco Vito, Rector of the Università del S. Cuore in Milan. A generous grant from the Relm Foundation made the research for the book, both here and in Europe, financially possible.

Mrs. Elinor Briefs, Mrs. Margaret McFadden, and my son Francis read the manuscript in its various drafts and made valuable editorial suggestions. Still others must be thanked for having been helpful in one way or another, particularly the graduate students at Georgetown University who attended my seminar in Advanced Economic Theory during 1961–62 when parts of the manuscript were under discussion. The unlimited support of my generous wife and helpful children sustained me throughout the labors that went into this book.

I owe this book to the opportunities given me at Georgetown University. May the book, published in the year of Georgetown's 175th anniversary, be a small contribution to the reality of the anniversary year's theme, "Wisdom and Discovery for a Dynamic World."

C. A. Zebot

Georgetown University
Washington, D.C.
March, 1964

CONTENTS

The Economics of Competitive Coexistence

CONVERGENCE THROUGH GROWTH